Praise for Practical Happiness

"*Practical Happiness* is a valuable guide to help you raise your happiness 'set point.' Pamela Gail Johnson offers four powerful principles along with transformational techniques you can easily apply in your life."

—**Marci Shimoff,** #1 *New York Times* bestselling author of *Happy for No Reason* and *Chicken Soup for the Woman's Soul*

"As a tour guide on the journey to happiness, Pamela Gail Johnson is good company. And more importantly, she knows the way. *Practical Happiness* is warm and wise and worth your time"

—**David Niven, Ph.D.,** bestselling author of *The 100 Simple Secrets of Happy People*

"If happiness is a habit, practicing Pamela Gail Johnson's principles are the roadmap to more fulfillment and well-being. Her book is full of real stories about real people putting her strategies into practice for a happier work and home life."

—**Nir Eyal,** bestselling author of *Indistractable: How to Control Your Attention and Choose V ife*

"I love the 4 principles of practical ha
Truly a fresh take on how to be h
highly enough!"

—**MJ Ryan,** bestselling . *..keover, Attitudes of Gratitude,* and 3 *.piness Boosters* among other titles

"Want to know why we find happy people annoying? Because they don't fully understand what happiness is. They think it's about ALWAYS being happy, upbeat, cheerful, and chipper. So, they fake it. The faking is what annoys us. Pamela has given us a way to be happy and to mean it. Practically. Realistically. Authentically. And while we will not always be happy in every moment, at least we can be happy consistently and with meaning. Give this book to someone as a gift and you could be giving them the gift of real happiness. Who knows? Maybe that person is yourself."

—**Tim David,** author of *Magic Words, The Four Levels of Influencing People,* and *The 7-Day Digital Diet*

"*Practical Happiness* is a well-researched, yet applicable method to taking charge of your own happiness and bettering your life."

—**David Burkus,** author of *Leading from Anywhere, Friend of a Friend,* and *Myths of Creativity*

"Pamela Gail Johnson's *Practical Happiness* is a practically perfect resource for understanding, recognizing, and building happiness in your life. She includes demonstrations of how happiness can be personal and enables the reader to find their own personal happiness inducers. She explains how to manage 'happiness zappers' and even create a personal 'zap map' to navigate them. She explores how happiness changes as we change, and helps us know how to help our happiness grow with us.

And she helps you explore how you experience thirty-one different types of happiness, and expand your experience of each of them. With her personal, easy-to-digest, highly readable tone, Johnson walks you through all the ways in which happiness is an inside job, and how you can get more happiness inside of yourself. This page-turner is packed with wisdom you can put to use right now."

—**Elizabeth Scott, PhD,** author of *8 Keys to Stress Management* and founder of *TranquilityTools.com*

"*Practical Happiness: Four Principles to Improve Your Life,* is a wonderful book! It is filled with simple ways to increase your happiness. Read this book and be happier!"

—**Mike Duffy,** author of *The Happiness Book: A Positive Guide To Happiness* and Founder of The Happiness Hall Of Fame

"The emotionally-charged stories Pamela shares from interviewing dozens of people who chose 'to be happy no matter what' give all of us deeper understanding of 'real' happiness in practical terms that can be easily applied to every-day life."

—**Dennis Yu,** host of the Coach Yu Show

"Pamela Johnson walks her talk. I did TV news stories on her two decades ago and since then, her mission to spread happiness and educate people on how to 'dial up the smile' has gone around the planet. This book is packed with actionable items that anyone can easily implement. The stress of the pandemic has made this book more necessary now than ever."

—**Jeff Crilley,** former Emmy Award winning reporter and CEO of Real News PR

"A great read for anyone who is looking for practical tips and strategies to create more happiness in their lives. Pamela allows you to take a different approach to creating your happiness, and shares stories that are relatable and inspiring."

—**Michelle Wax,** founder, American Happiness Project

"The four principles taught in *Practical Happiness* are so simple to apply. I love that it has a fill-in-the blank workbook style so you can take action while you read. Read this with a pen if you're ready to smile again."

—**Jeff J. Hunter,** founder of VAStaffer.com and creator of the CORE Branding Method

"Pursuing happiness is the most basic of human objectives but yet one that can remain elusive. In a time where languishing seems more the norm than flourishing, what could be timelier than a pragmatic perspective on how to cultivate happiness! Pamela has created a practical guide to build a skill that is crucial to enhance our individual life experience and our collective energy of gratitude and optimism."

—**Susan Sobbott,** board member, senior advisor, and former American Express President of OPEN, GCP, GCS

PRACTICAL HAPPINESS

Four Principles to Improve Your Life

PAMELA GAIL JOHNSON
Founder, Society of Happy People

Health Communications, Inc.
Boca Raton, Florida

www.hcibooks.com

Library of Congress Cataloging-in-Publication Data
is available through the Library of Congress

ISBN-13: 978-07573-2413-0 (Paperback)
ISBN-10: 07573-2413-4 (Paperback)
ISBN-13: 978-07573-2414-7 (ePub)
ISBN-10: 0-7573-2414-2 (ePub)

Publisher: Health Communications, Inc.
1700 NW 2nd Avenue
Boca Raton, FL 33432-1653

Cover design by Larissa Hise Henoch
Interior design by Larissa Hise Henoch, formatting by Lawna Patterson Oldfield
Author photo credit Juli Santizo

For all of the souls who've crossed my path . . .

Thank you for the happy
moments we've shared,
the difficult times you've
helped me through,
and the lessons you've
taught me that have
helped me become more
compassionate, wiser, and
even happier.

CONTENTS

ACKNOWLEDGMENTS

When I founded the Society of Happy People more than twenty years ago, it changed my life in ways that I could never have imagined.

I always wanted to make the world a better place. The Society has given me the opportunity to do that. It has been an honor to connect with so many others who are doing the same thing.

It's also impossible to thank everyone individually who's been part of the journey that has influenced this book. So, first, I want to thank the unnamed who have inspired my heart.

A very special thank-you goes to Sean Giggy, the television reporter at WFAA in Dallas–Fort Worth who asked me in an interview, "What have you learned about happiness in the past twenty years?" That one question motivated me to reexamine and give even more life to *Practical Happiness* and its four principles.

And thank you, Jeff Crilley, for getting me that interview, among many others, and for also being so supportive of me and the Society of Happy People from the beginning.

Next, I want to thank my agent, Linda Konner, who saw the wisdom of this book and helped me make the message stronger.

Also, many thanks to the HCI Books team—Christine Belleris, Christian Blonshine, Larissa Henoch, Allison Janse, Bob Land, Lindsey Mach, Camilla Michael, and Lawna Patterson Oldfield—for sharing my vision for this book and being a delight to work with.

The heart of *Practical Happiness* comes from the stories shared by so many people. My heartfelt thanks to everyone who generously shared their stories that demonstrated the four happiness principles and showed us how a practical approach to happiness helps everyone live a happier life: Anna-Sophia Adam, Grissette Alvarado, Sheila Best, Tom Bloomer, Chester Boyd, Kami Bumgardner, Martha Burich, Lupe Centeno, Allyson Chavez, Thomas Cluck, Cassandra Cooper, Kim Corbin, Paula Crandall, Ariana DeFreitas, Kristin DeFreitas, Gretchen Dixon, Justin Dorsey, Norman Terrill Fischer, Kelliann Flores, Yvette Francino, Shalisa Holmes Graham, Richard Greene, Karen Haller, Janice Hathy, Leslee Loving Herald, Ferrell Hornsby, Remberto "Rem" Jimenez, Kay Johnson, Genny Jones, Vickie Keith, Jackson Kerchis, Jennifer Kuehn, Hillary Lackore, Kari

Lackore, Hema Lakkaraju, Jeff Lenhart, Francisco Mahfuz, Sharon Markman, Maureen McElligott, Rose Mis, Anna Morgan, Apryl Motely, Rae Mowry, Chantal Naidoo, Robert Potillo, Ganesh Ramaswamy, Amy Ramon, Uno Sandvik, Elizabeth Scott, Jovon Selby, Alex Sheridan, Karen Silins, Debbie Sanders Simon, Nichole Smith, Toby Smith, Yaacov Steinberg, Brianne Swisher, Crystal Synger (Rebecca), Maureen Way, Michelle Wax, Lisa White, Robin Williams, and Dennis Yu.

It was impossible to include all the great nuggets of wisdom shared by these contributors, so if anyone's story inspired you, visit sohp.com/phc to connect with them and their happiness wisdom.

I'm so grateful that I professionally crossed paths many years ago with my now friend and writing mentor, Nina L. Diamond. She helped shape this book, thanks to our many conversations and her editorial advice.

Also, thank you, Kristen McGuiness, for helping to craft my book proposal.

Juli Santizo, thank you for your patience taking my author photo.

Several years ago, I started a fiction book club. Although I knew I'd have fun in the book club, I never realized how much I'd learn from listening to everyone discuss the books. My book club made me a better writer, so thank you to Victoria Boyd, Jennifer Keuhn, Kari Lackore, Kathi Shaw, and Jill Whetstone.

Of course, none of this is possible without those who have helped shape and define the Society. David Perry's original logo is still timeless and makes people smile decades later. Bob Wieland's Associated Press story gave the Society credibility in our early days, and his continued friendship over the years has been so valuable. Juan Paulo Olandez's intuitive ability to read my mind leads him to create beautiful Society graphics that are even better than I could imagine.

Thank you to Rose Mis for making sure that the Society has a wonderful online presence, and for being my tech mind. She is a wonderful professional collaborator and an even better friend.

A special thanks to Tim David for helping me turn the message of this book into speeches.

Life is so much happier when you get to work with people who make you smile.

And, finally, to all my friends and family who've dreamed this book with me, who have kept my spirits up when I experienced Happiness Zappers, and who inspire every day: Tonna Amos, Javier and Lupe Centeno, Christine Delorey, Mini Dority, Annie Garza, Kay Johnson, Jennifer Jolly, William Monif, Linda Moore, Rae Mowry, Cindy and Robert Reddoor, Beth Varma, Mary and Mike Voigt, and Cristina Younes.

And while they are no longer here with us, I have to thank

my late parents for providing the foundation for the person I am today: Mary Lafferty Denhart and Jerry Johnson. Also, my aunt Barbara Lafferty for always supporting my dreams. And my dog, Tater, my furry soulmate who was the center of my happiness for years.

This book is brought to you by so many people who have shaped my life. It's truly humbling and makes my heart beat a little faster simply thinking of them. I'm blessed to know so many loving and uplifting people.

I'm excited to meet more of you who read this book and expand my connections with even more happy people.

As always, sending you peace, love, and happiness.

INTRODUCTION

A Native American story tells about how God gathered his animal advisers together, to help him decide where to hide the Secret to a Happy Life from humans.

He first asked the Eagle, "Where shall I put it?"

The Eagle answered, "I shall hide it at the top of the highest mountain. Man will never find it there."

God considered this but decided against it. "One day, Man will go there," he said.

Next, he asked the Clam, "Where shall I put it, little Clam?"

"I will hide it at the bottom of the deepest ocean," the Clam answered.

This seemed like a better idea, but the Lord hesitated again. "Man will go there someday," he said after some thought.

Then the wise Owl stepped forward. "Though I regretfully cannot take it there myself," he intoned, "perhaps you ought to hide the secret on the moon."

After considering this, God finally came to the same conclusion as before: "No. There, too, Man shall go."

After some period of reflection, the humble Opossum came forward. "Perhaps," he said, so softly that he could barely be heard, "the secret should be hidden in the heart of Man." There was an awed silence among the animals.

Finally, the Lord spoke: "Yes, cunning Opossum, that will be the last place Man will look."

This story reminds us of something that we already know but are often reluctant to embrace: Our happiness is inside us. The challenge is knowing how to find it.

The problem? *Our brains are hardwired to quickly recognize and help us get away from things that can hurt us.* This goes back to our caveman days, when we had to protect ourselves from gigantic, hairy, scary creatures and such. Our brains evolved to help us recognize danger and keep us safe. That's why it's always easier, and maybe even more natural, for us to see what's wrong before we can see what's right. Having a positive outlook usually requires a conscious effort until it becomes a habit or our go-to mindset.

Most of us are also culturally conditioned to think *we'll be happy when* we get the next bright, shiny new thing on our I'll Be Happy When List. You know what I'm talking about: that dream career, that oh-so-lovable pet, that super-sexy/super-fast dream car, that gorgeous spouse, the big house, the perfect kids, the vacations in Europe, a healthy financial portfolio; the list goes on and on. It's not that these things don't contribute to your happiness, but their mere acquisition only offers fleeting tastes of it. It's like when you decide to binge-watch a season of reality TV: the moments you watched were entertaining, fun, and amusing, but twelve hours later, you wonder if there was a better use of your time.

Happiness from your I'll Be Happy When List is directly related to the experiences you have in achieving those goals. Humans are very contradictory beings! Instead of recognizing that our happiest moments often happen on the way to the destination, we instead take them for granted, believing that the goal is the ultimate happiness prize. We fail to recognize the happiness we experience in our efforts to achieve our dreams, which is why their attainment can leave us feeling empty, making us believe that we need to find our next "I'll be happy when."

A few years after graduating from college, a friend reached the point financially where he could buy his dream car: a really hot, limited-edition Corvette. Initially, he was excited when he drove his car, looking for any opportunity to take it out for a spin. But within a short time, his dream car simply became his transportation. It ceased being special because it was part of his normal day. Did the car change? No. Did the experience of driving it change? No. But his *perception* of driving it did. The car quit being special because it was now ordinary. Could driving his dream car be part of his daily happiness? Of course, but that would depend on his happiness mindset.

A house doesn't make you happy. The experiences that happen inside the house are what make it a home. Homes, not houses, are your source of happiness because they are filled with memories created with your beloved family, your friends, and your pets.

Happiness is rarely an outside job. It's when we look inside our homes, our relationships, and our lives that we find it hiding there. That's why a specific job title won't make you happy; the experiences you get to have as a result of that title lead to your professional happiness.

Likewise, an engagement ring doesn't make you happy. It's the experience of loving someone enough to commit to building a life together that produces your happiness.

Happiness is a lot easier to find than we've given it credit for, which is the real secret of practical happiness.

So, what is *practical happiness*? It's the foundation for *realistic* happiness. It means expecting that unhappiness, stress, fear, chaos, and annoyances will zap your happiness sometimes while trusting that you can manage these Happiness Zappers. It's understanding that happiness is unique for each of us, yet the experiences that make us happy are fluid and change. It's recognizing that happiness is the rush of *excitement* but also the serenity of *contentment* and the many other types of happiness in between—thirty-one of them, in fact.

I formalized the four practical happiness principles after a TV reporter, Sean Giggy of WFAA in Dallas–Fort Worth, interviewed me when the Society of Happy People turned twenty. He asked, "What have you learned about happiness in the past twenty years?"

When I thought about it, a few important insights stood out. One of them involved me personally. Some people assume that I'm happy all the time. But no one, not even the founder of the Society of Happy People, is happy *all* the time. I'd certainly experienced my share of unhappiness, stress, fear, chaos, and annoyances—Happiness Zappers. Both of my mom's parents, whom I adored, passed away when I was in my early teens. My mother was in a serious car accident that took her almost three years to recover from when I was in high school. My parents divorced during my senior year of college. I didn't always have the money for everything I wanted or needed. And, of course, my heart was broken multiple times through the years, just to mention a few of my significant Happiness Zappers.

However, I've always been naturally optimistic. I believe that everything, the good and the bad, happens for a reason. Our purpose is to try to learn lessons from both. So when Sean asked what I'd learned about happiness since creating the Society, I realized that my happiness wasn't about specific experiences but rather how I allowed those experiences to define my happiness.

One of the biggest lessons I learned in those two decades is that we don't always get to choose what our life looks like. Of course, some of our choices impact it, but often life happens, and we need to adjust our dreams. We lose old ones and discover new ones. Often, our biggest choice is how we react to our experiences because our happiness changes when we change.

Long after Sean asked me that question, I kept thinking about it. I reread things I had written in Society newsletters and my responses to emails and social media posts from the early days of the Society to the present. There was an ongoing theme: I always wanted people to experience more—yet realistic—happiness, and that didn't mean pretending Happiness Zappers didn't happen or that we could wish them away. It did mean, however, shifting our happiness mindset.

Here's an example: Very few people think, *I can't wait to clean out my garage*. You probably procrastinate about doing it. Then one weekend you can't find something you need, so you decide it's finally time to organize the garage. Of course, the actual act of cleaning out and reorganizing your garage probably doesn't make you smile. It's yucky, dirty, overwhelming work. You'd rather be doing a million other things. But after you've finished cleaning out and organizing your garage, you probably feel many types of happiness. *Relieved* that it's finally done. *Satisfied* that you can find what you need. And if you donated some unwanted items, you felt happiness from *giving* to others. So an experience that you didn't perceive as happy is actually connected to many types of happiness. It's all about how you think about it, your happiness mindset, and practicing *practical happiness*.

I began to realize that everyone could access happiness at almost any time if they were able to recognize some simple realistic principles about how happiness worked. With that goal in mind, I came up with the four practical happiness principles:

- Happiness is personal.
- Happiness Zappers can be managed.
- Happiness changes as you change.
- Happiness is bigger than you think.

Looking back, I realized that these principles defined my practical happiness mindset.

Shortly after my mom passed away in 2004, I wanted to get a dog. When I mentioned it to my then boyfriend, he didn't like the idea. But then, a couple of months after the one-year anniversary of my mother's passing, my brother, who lived nearby, sent me a picture of his new puppy. I was so excited because I unexpectedly became a puppy-sitting aunt. I'd get the best of both worlds, puppy love without puppy ownership.

When my brother took Tater to his first vet visit, he was diagnosed with a severe heart problem. It ultimately required two surgeries at Texas A&M, years of follow-up visits, and a couple of years of daily medicine given on a very strict schedule. He could have had a heart attack if a dose of medication was missed at the appropriate times.

My brother and I agreed to share Tater so that his medical issues could be properly managed. I fell head over heels in love with this high-maintenance and medically expensive dog. My life changed to the point that my brother and I even bought townhomes on the same street to make it easier to share Tater.

Tater unexpectedly changed my life and what made me happy. Even though his health issues provided many Happiness Zappers, they proved to be manageable. Ultimately, Tater introduced me to many types of happiness. Obviously, he filled my heart with *love,* and after every positive vet appointment I felt *relief.* Each day we *played,* and his presence brought me *joy.* Tater is a perfect example of practicing practical happiness and its four principles.

Since the Society started, there has been a huge increase in happiness-science studies. While it's good to know that happiness has a scientific foundation, my own experience is that your happiness begins with your mindset. Your happiness mindset comes from how you perceive and stay present for what is happening right now. Happiness can defy science, or even a step-by-step process, when you have a practical happiness mindset, which means taking the time to notice all the happiness in your life in real time.

As the founder of the Society of Happy People, I've interacted with thousands of happy people and happiness seekers. I've learned from them that without the correct mindset, you probably won't or can't find much happiness. And we all want to feel more happiness because, quite simply, it feels good. Yet happiness can also feel elusive. Many people believe they can only feel happiness in the absence of conflict. But happy moments happen during even the most challenging times. Sometimes happiness can be harder to notice than at other times, like when you've lost someone you love, you experience economic hardships, or your life becomes constricted because of a global health pandemic.

For this reason, it is even more important that we stay focused on our happy experiences when we experience either life-changing events or many Happiness Zappers simultaneously; we must balance our feelings so that the unpleasant ones do not overtake the happy ones that are often hiding in plain sight.

Ironically, when things are going well, we can also fall into the trap of taking most of our everyday happy moments for granted. When we fail to notice them, we also miss the chance to be present with them—or sometimes we may minimize our happiness because we are afraid that it will go away, so our fear of loss becomes more significant than our happy experience.

Sometimes, when we expect an experience will make us happy, it doesn't meet our expectations. And yet, at other times, an experience that we didn't think would make us feel good provides an abundance of happiness. Our expectations of happiness can make it elusive, yet when we let ourselves just experience the moment, happiness can surprise us.

Practical Happiness is here to help you whether your happiness feels sparse, abundant, or somewhere in-between. This book is filled with stories from and about people showing the four practical happiness principles in action. It recognizes the realities of life's challenges, including the ones that make you feel stressed, anxious, and fearful, and helps you to shift your mindset so that you naturally notice happiness whether you are experiencing the best or worst of times.

Principle One: HAPPINESS IS PERSONAL

Since I started the Society of Happy People in 1998, I'm often asked in media interviews, "What makes you happy?"

I've always answered, "That really depends on my mood. If I've had a busy day, curling up with a great book is happiness. If I've been consumed by work, dinner with friends makes me happy. If I've been traveling, a kiss from my dog is my happy highlight. And right now, it's talking to you about happiness."

I've always believed that happiness is personal—it's also based on what recharges your happiness batteries in that moment. The difference between happiness and pleasure is your mindset. Pleasure makes you feel good, but it's fleeting. After that moment, you could very well go back to feeling as you did before that moment of pleasure. Happiness makes you feel good for longer. Although not all happy moments provide the same energetic high, the good feelings recharge your soul or your happiness battery, so you do benefit from that happy experience for a longer time.

THE SCIENCE OF HAPPINESS

Since the research from the positive psychology movement was initially released in 1998, many scientific studies have been conducted about what makes us happy. While the conclusions in these studies are important, they are not the only factors in determining our happiness.

My friend Gretchen was helping take care of my beloved yet high-maintenance dog, Tater, while I was traveling. At that time, Gretchen happened to be going through many Happiness Zappers simultaneously: divorce discussions with her husband, job displacement, taking care of her mom, and mourning a friend who'd passed away. She was stressed out, and while all of these situations would resolve with time, she was having very few happy experiences at that point.

Naturally I wanted to help, so on a couple of occasions before leaving for my trips, I said, "I have some lavender oil if you'd like to diffuse it or put it on your temples. Scientifically, it's been proven to help with stress. I realize lavender oil won't resolve the actual issues causing the stress, but it might give you a little relief." She politely declined.

Finally, after the third time I offered, she kindly smiled and said, "The smell of lavender makes me want to throw up." I started laughing out loud because I'd been so far off the mark.

Obviously, it didn't matter if lavender scents helped 99 out of 100 people reduce their stress. If it makes you want to throw up, that's not a stress reliever for you. The science doesn't matter, so when we look at the science of happiness, we also have to look at how it pertains to each of us.

Countless studies confirm runners get a runner's high. Running triggers all our feel-good chemicals. Although the thought of completing a marathon makes me smile, nothing feels happy to me about running, sweating, and sweating some more. Despite the scientific benefits of running, that activity doesn't feel happy to me.

Our happiness is more personal than scientific.

COMPONENTS OF HAPPINESS

Dr. Sonja Lyubomirsky led a Stanford study that shows three factors that affect our happiness are: genetics, circumstances, and activities.

Alex Sheridan, a social media brand expert, told me, "My natural state is to be positive and happy. It makes me the perfect entrepreneur because I can get punched in the face twenty times, get knocked down every single day, and I'm still going to have a smile on my face. You just can't keep me down. As long as my kids are good and healthy, I'm going to keep moving forward. If I get knocked down, it's an opportunity to learn something, then get back up again.

"Discipline is a big part of my happiness," he continued. "The more disciplined you are around what you want to accomplish and the things you need to do, the prouder you feel about yourself and the direction you're going. It makes you more accomplished, which makes your life turn out better. If you say you're going to spend time with your kids, then be present in the moment, and do it. If you say you're going to put time into your business because you want to grow it, then do that. If you say you're going to work out and eat healthy because that makes you feel and look better, and have better health, then do it. For me, discipline leads to happiness."

Although Alex naturally experiences a high degree of happiness, he also knows his actions contribute to his happiness.

Others are born with biological happiness challenges. They simply don't have a high genetic happiness set point. Some people manage ongoing depression, anxiety, or other mental health challenges. Some people deal with chronic pain and ongoing medical issues that make it difficult to physically feel good. And everyone can experience situational depression and anxiety.

Ariana, who manages ongoing depression and anxiety, said, "It's really nice to look back and find the happy spots, even in the days when it was dark for me. I could see this continual thread of happiness that runs through my life. Sometimes I had to look for it and point it out, and remind myself that it's there, even when it's not in the forefront at that moment. But I think there's something really powerful about talking about happiness, and reminiscing, and seeing it in the past, seeing it in the present, and knowing that it's going to be there in the future.

"Understanding my emotions and experiences and then choosing happiness helps," she continued. "I learned that I get a lot of my energy and my spirit from being around people and feeling supported and supporting others. So I think a lot of my happiness stems from being in a community as well."

Dogs make Ariana personally happy. She grew up with them from the time she was a baby. When she moved from Dallas to Seattle, adopting a dog was her number-one priority. It took about two years, but she finally got her dog.

"It felt like Birdie was waiting for me, and I was waiting for her," said Ariana. "When my fiancé and I moved in together, we felt like it was time to get a dog. We moved in together when the pandemic started, so tons of dogs got adopted in Seattle, and we couldn't find one. We finally found one in Montana. Initially, we put a deposit down for Birdie's sister. When we arrived at the shelter we asked if we could meet both puppies. We expected to get the sister, but Birdie had it in her mind that we were her family. She came up and sat right down in my lap, and was all snuggly and cuddly. Her sister didn't really care and was just running around peeing all over the place. Birdie gave us a ton of attention. We both looked at each other and were like *This is our dog*. It's like she picked us. We switched and adopted her. It felt like she was waiting for us in Montana.

"A lot of my happiness stems from having a dog companion who has really strong emotions and understands my emotions and reacts to them in a very comforting way," she added.

COMPETITIVE HAPPINESS

Another factor that influences our personal happiness is *competitive happiness*. In the 1950s, it was called "keeping up with the Joneses." It's natural to compare what we have, or what makes us happy, to others. Sometimes this inspires us. But it can also foster jealousy that zaps our happiness. The amount of happiness that we get from identical experiences or things won't be the same as someone else. It might be more. It might be less. It will be personal to us.

The year that I started the Society of Happy People, Ann Landers wrote in her Thanksgiving weekend column that people shouldn't send happy holiday newsletters in their greeting cards. (This was when the majority of people mailed holiday cards.) She basically told people not to share their happy news because it might make someone else feel bad. The Society issued a press release saying that people had a right to share their happy news in holiday letters, and international news outlets wrote about it. Her column and our response initially launched the Society's platform that people had a right to talk about being happy if they were happy. Sharing your happiness isn't about making someone feel bad; it's about elevating the energy of everyone to feel better.

Fast-forward to the era of social media, and everyone's annual happy holiday newsletters have become their daily posts with pictures for their family and friends. Naturally, some people compare their lives to posts shared. They also compare who liked or commented on posts. If the post is happy, some assume your whole life is happy. Or if they know you experience Happiness Zappers, they decide your post isn't about an authentic happy moment. Now we can even compare our happiness to people we don't know—the social media influencers. Social media has made it easy to participate in competitive happiness if that is where our mindset wants to go, but there are no winners in this competition.

"I consider social media to be happiness neutral," Dennis Yu, an online social media expert, told me. "It's like technology:

'Is technology good or bad?' It depends on how you use it. 'Is fire good or bad?' You can use fire to cook a delicious steak, or you can burn yourself.

"Recently I had dinner with one of my teammates," added Dennis. "We took some pictures to post on Instagram, but our Korean barbeque started to get cold. And the joke was, well, the 'Gram eats first.' We wanted to highlight that moment and share it with other people. There's nothing wrong with sharing that completely authentic moment. The risk is that sometimes you spend so much effort capturing the moment that you lose the moment itself. I've done that. As a tourist at Disneyland, I really wanted to capture that special moment with Mickey Mouse so much that I forgot that I needed to really focus on the time that I was spending with the people who I was with, and treasure those relationships, and have a balance between the actual experience and the time I spent capturing it. A lot of people don't know how to create that balance, especially young adults.

"Never before have people had to find a balance between their real life and this digital life," Dennis continued. "The older generations didn't have to do that. The camera was something that was turned on only when there was a wedding or some kind of important moment like graduation. It was expensive, like twenty-five cents for every picture. Now it's flipped, and by default, the camera is on all the time. So that's a huge shift between generations. And only the younger one has had to experience pictures and videos being taken twenty-four seven. I think that's creating confusion because people still have only twenty-four hours in a day, but now they have to manage both a real and multichannel digital life. Managing all of these channels creates a problem of overwhelm. It's not that the technology is bad. It's not that social media is evil. We can use it for good, but we have to train people to understand why they are using it."

Social media has increased our ability to participate in competitive happiness, but it's also made it much easier to share the events that make us happy and inspire us with the people we love. Fortunately, *we can control how much time we spend on social media*. We can decide which posts receive our attention. We can ignore the posts that annoy us. But it might be worth asking why a post annoys us in the first place, especially if it was shared by someone we know personally.

Since our happiness is personal, it doesn't need to be competitive. *There is enough happiness for everyone.* After all, do you want to focus on someone else's happiness or your own?

WHAT MAKES OTHERS PERSONALLY HAPPY

The experiences that make us feel good and happy have commonalities with others, yet each one is a little unique to us. For example, millions of people may feel inspired by the same song, but each person may interpret it a little differently; therefore, its meaning is unique to them. Here are a few ways that others find their unique personal happiness. They might inspire you to find yours, too.

Ferrell, Utah

"I love nature," said Ferrell. "That's a real personal happiness for me. In fact, I recently started setting my alarm for when the sun sets so that I can go outside and watch it. It's a very personal moment for me to watch the glories of those sunsets."

Francisco, Spain

"I dislike the idea of looking forward to things," said Francisco. "I think a lot of people look forward to the weekend, holidays, or a great party. One of the things that made me much happier, over the last ten or more years, was trying to find the happiness in every little moment of my day. I really don't look ahead much. I feel that shortchanges the next minute, or hour, or day, if I'm looking forward to the next big thing. I believe that the next happy moment is what's coming up immediately. This has made it a lot simpler to find happiness that I might miss if I'm just looking for the next big thing."

Genny, Great Britain

When people tell Genny that she always seems so happy and positive, she responds, "Every morning, I spend an hour fueling myself. I don't wake up the happiest, so I have a morning routine. I pray. I meditate. I listen to something inspirational. I might go for a walk. And then I set my intentions, *Today is a good day. I am going to have a happy day.* I set myself up for the day in the morning. I do the same thing before I go to sleep. I review the day, and go to bed with good thoughts. I do these things every single day to keep myself in a happiness mindset."

Hema, California

"My happiness comes from the sense of freedom that my work as an author, speaker, and entrepreneur gives me," said Hema. "I can innovate and be the leader of my own time. I can define where I spend the time, and that is true happiness for me. I get to enjoy the freedom of taking a walk in the middle of the day and helping my kids with projects or at their school activities."

Justin, Texas

"I find a lot of happiness from being outside on the weekends," Justin, an HR professional, explained. "I enjoy working with my hands, digging in the dirt, and playing with vegetables. Doing anything outside brings me joy. It's funny because when you look back on your childhood, a lot of these things were like chores: 'Go mow the yard,' or 'Sweep the porch.' Now I find myself enjoying these things. They give me a sense of completion and accomplishment. Some things I do at work feel like there is really no end to them. They're just kind of perpetually happening. And there's always more to be done. They never reach the point, like yardwork does, where I can look back and say, 'Oh, the grass looks good.' This gives me a sense of happiness."

Leslee, Texas

The ending of Leslee's twenty-five-year marriage was the catalyst that helped her truly understand happiness. "I began to realize how unhappy I was in that marriage," she shared. "I started going to therapy to find myself again and found happiness along the way. I started taking little day trips by myself. That's when I realized that I really enjoyed nature. I started taking pictures of flowers and appreciating nature. They made me feel calm and happy. Now I like to get into the car, only knowing I'm going north, south, east, or west. But beyond that, I don't know where I'm going. I just drive, listening to great music. Then I stop along the way when I see some flowers, cows, or horses. I may pet them or take pictures. Sometimes I just stop and sit on the side of the road to take in everything."

Lisa, Illinois

Although she's still dealing with depression and complex PTSD, after ending a traumatic ten-year marriage, Lisa explained, "I find happiness from learning new things. I'm like a sponge, and it excites me. Also, when I'm successful in the tiniest, tiniest tasks. I filled a hole in the wall with a little bit of putty, and it made me happy. It's small, but because of where I'm at in my life, knowing that I succeeded at even a small thing makes me happy. I'm digging out of an emotional hole. So teeny-tiny things make me happy. It was like Christmas when I recently ordered my first Keurig coffeemaker. Right now, my happiness comes from little baby steps. And my dog. He's been a real lifesaver."

Dennis, Nevada

Dennis, who gets about a thousand emails a day, said, "This is gonna sound silly, but if you're a programmer, you'll appreciate it. I really like getting to Inbox Zero, to clear out all my messages across Twitter, Facebook, email, and text. It's like a game, and the challenge is to get down to zero. Do you ever check your phone, see three notifications, and you just want to clear it so it disappears? That's sort of the contest that I have with myself where I feel that if I do this, I win the message game. I want to finish. I don't want to leave things 90 percent done. Sometimes I reply to emails at two in the morning, just because I want to get that inbox done."

Michelle, Massachusetts

"I love waking up early and going for a walk when the sun's rising," said Michelle. "I know for so many people that sounds miserable. But for me, whenever I wake up early and take time to get outside, I just feel like the day is set up so much better. It is a refreshing and amazing start to the day."

Sheila, California

"One of the things that makes me happiest is clean sheets on my bed," Sheila, who's retired, told me. "I put them on my bed at least once a week, sometimes more. I love crawling into bed because they smell so good. I'm also a foodie, so making myself a nice meal makes me happy. I do it four or five times a week. I always have my dining room table set with a placemat and a cloth napkin. I like to eat nicely. During the day, I'll carry around a plastic bottle of water, but when I sit down for my meal, I use glasses, china plates, and nice silverware. There's no reason to not have nice things or to set things up nicely for yourself."

Maureen, Canada

"Dancing puts me in a joyful mood and connects me to Spirit," Maureen shared. "It's a way to express all of the emotions that you can't say with words."

Vickie, Texas

"I am a Zumba instructor," explained Vickie, who's retired. "My sister-in-law took me to my first class in 2009 when I weighed 213 pounds, and I fell in love with it. I could barely get through it because I was in such bad shape. However, I kept going back because I loved it. Over the course of fifteen months, I lost 82 pounds and got my instructor's license. It took me two years to get over my fear of teaching. I didn't think that I would be a very good teacher. At my age, I didn't think I'd be able to remember the routines. My friend tricked me into teaching my first class. Once I taught that class, I've taught ever since. It makes me so happy. I love teaching. I love my ladies. I love seeing them transform from that person in the back row to the front-row diva."

Yaacov, Israel

"I like adult coloring books," Yaacov said. "I even posted one that I colored on LinkedIn. Coloring lets me zone out so that I can just fill in the lines and create something beautiful, something I really appreciate."

Now it's your turn. While it's easy to understand that our happiness is personal, we don't always think of it that way. While we appreciate when something makes us feel good or happy in the moment, we may not acknowledge it for longer than the moment in which it happens. When we practice practical happiness, we need to recognize the experiences that make us happy most of the time. That way, when we need to boost our happiness, we have go-to actions that we know will make us feel better.

What are five things on your Happiness Is Personal List? Consider what people shared earlier about what makes them happy. Your Happiness Is Personal List may include things as simple as taking a walk, talking to your bestie, or cooking. Or it may be as complex as a multitask morning routine.

Happiness Is Personal List
1.
2.
3.
4.
5.

When we are happier, we naturally notice more happiness in others and in life. Our vibe naturally rises, and we attract more experiences that make us feel good.

Let's have a little fun. Find out how happy you are with the Society of Happy People's *"You Might Be a Happy Person If . . . Checklist"* at sohp.com/phhp.

Principle Two: HAPPINESS ZAPPERS ARE MANAGEABLE

It happens all the time. When anyone finds out that I founded the Society of Happy People, they automatically think I believe everyone should always be happy. I find that quite amusing because nothing could be further from the truth. Even though I'd love to be part of a happy, high-vibe-only world, it's just not a realistic dream, hope, or expectation.

Happiness Zappers are those moments that lower our energy and then distract us from recognizing our happy experiences. They happen to everyone. Even when we experience Happiness Zappers, we still have moments of happiness, too. Sometimes we don't notice them, and other times we just take them for granted.

We often wonder why it's so much easier to notice our unhappiness than happiness. In part, our brains are hardwired to protect us from perceived danger. It's how we survived our caveman days and stayed alive. We were always on the lookout for wild animals, enough food, bad weather, and safe shelter. And while our physical survival is much less difficult now, we are constantly reminded about how scary the world can be, how we could improve or have more stuff, and basically that our life could be better. We also instinctively self-protect emotionally because we don't want to feel heartache, disappointment, or failure. Our instinctual self-protection makes it easier to recognize what's wrong at the expense of acknowledging what's right.

Studies even show that people who consider themselves mostly happy and those who consider themselves mostly unhappy experience about the same amount of happy and Happiness Zapper experiences. Therefore, how we manage our Happiness Zappers is a big factor in determining our overall happiness or unhappiness.

Many Happiness Zappers are common experiences: the death of a loved one, arguments with our kids, or health challenges that require lifestyle changes. Yet other Happiness Zappers are personal. One person might get annoyed with traffic jams and someone else might see them as opportunities to listen to their favorite podcasts. Happiness Zappers, like happiness, are unique to each of us.

When we've been drained by a Happiness Zapper, our emotions can range from frustration to anger to heartache. These feelings often appear bigger than any of the happiness we experience. They lower our vibe, which then changes how we feel and what we attract and create.

The biggest remedy for when you experience Happiness Zappers is to manage them so that you can feel better, even if it's just for a short moment. To add a little fun to managing Happiness Zappers, I think of it as creating a ZAP-MAP: a Zapper Management Action Plan, which we discuss in more detail later in this chapter.

When Paula was laid off from her fifth job within a few years, naturally she was very tired of this repeating happiness-zapping experience. However, she quickly went into ZAP-MAP mode. The day she was laid off, she gave herself the rest of the day to lick her wounds, feel sorry for herself, mourn, complain, and whine.

Then the next day, she said, "Okay, I've done this four times before. Looking back, it's always turned out okay. I always end up with another job, even if it wasn't always a great job. I've been able to pay my bills and keep food on the table."

She then went into action by reaching out to her support community to let them know what was going on: she needed spiritual and emotional support—and job leads.

Paula managed this Happiness Zapper initially by allowing

herself to feel her unhappy emotions because denying them didn't feel good. She knew they had to be released. Then she implemented her plan of action to get another job, which also made her feel good.

TYPES OF HAPPINESS ZAPPERS

The specific causes for Happiness Zappers vary, yet the common experiences can be put into these five categories: unhappiness, stress, fear, chaos, and annoyances.

Unhappiness is most often connected to loss when we must create a new normal over time. The death of someone or a pet we loved is the ultimate loss. Yet other losses redefine our lives, too: unwanted career changes, health challenges, friend or family conflicts, and other normal, expected, or even unexpected life changes.

Stress is when we feel pressure or tension from things that require a response from us that can impact us mentally, emotionally, physically, and spiritually.

Fear creates a physiological change that influences our behavior when we are actually threatened by a dangerous situation or we believe something may threaten our physical or emotional safety in the future.

Chaos happens when things are in disarray, unorganized, and confusing.

Annoyances are when someone or something irritates or bothers us to the point that our mood is adversely affected.

Managing our Happiness Zappers begins when we think about them a little differently.

Identify one or more Happiness Zappers from each zapper category you have experienced in the last twenty-four hours. If you have not experienced one for a particular category in that time, then list your most recent Happiness Zapper experience for that category. Try to include a different experience for each category.

Type of Happiness Zapper	Happiness Zapper Experience(s)
Unhappiness	
Stress	
Fear	
Chaos	
Annoyances	

Obviously, you may experience more than one Happiness Zapper at the same time for the same situation. For example, when your alarm doesn't go off and you start your morning late, getting yourself and your family ready for the day may be both chaotic and stressful. Yet ultimately the situation creates only brief chaos that you can manage pretty quickly, although the stress from that moment may linger.

Unhappiness

It's easy to think all Happiness Zappers create unhappiness. But the difference between unhappiness and the other Happiness Zappers is that it comes from situations that require us to take time to find a new normal and, often, involve grieving a loss. It may even be one of the catalysts for the third principle: "Happiness Changes As You Change." The other Happiness Zappers are usually managed in a shorter amount of time and rarely require us to find a new normal.

When we experience unhappiness, how we manage its longer-lasting ebbs and flows determines how that experience ultimately impacts us. Is it a bridge for growth that may include developing more compassion and empathy for others? Or does the experience become a justification to stay distraught with hurt and anger?

Managing unhappiness doesn't mean denying when we feel bad. We actually have to feel our way through it. When we don't embrace this process, we're at risk of drowning in our bad feelings. We still need to allow ourselves to feel the good moments when they happen. Sometimes when we experience unhappiness, we can feel guilty when we allow ourselves to feel anything good. We think we should feel bad all the time because of a loss—or when life isn't turning out as we planned.

Unhappiness is simply a time that changes and shapes us. How it does that is up to us.

Nichole became an unexpected widow when she was thirty-eight after being married for fifteen years. Her husband died of an overdose. Although he had dealt with addiction issues before their dating and getting married, he didn't really struggle with them until the last year of their marriage.

After an already chaotic and difficult year of dealing with her husband's active addiction, Nichole unexpectedly found herself in the throes of grief—and a single parent to their four kids.

She says that what kept her going for the next few months was a mantra she played in her head: *Just take things one day, one hour, one minute, one second at a time.* "I just focused on the next second, and then on the next minute. I didn't look too far into the future. I did what I needed to do to get to the next step of the day. Sometimes that was simply reminding myself to eat, sleep, or even shower. It was just progress forward, no matter what."

She didn't let herself worry about the little annoyances or the chaos of the house.

During the last few months of her husband's life, they went to therapy. She shared, "My marriage was full of really high highs or low lows, and there wasn't much in the middle." However, she believes his death changed her happiness perspective.

A month before her husband's death, after finding reasons not to return to college, she finally enrolled so that she could achieve her twenty-year dream to graduate. Since she didn't qualify for scholarships, she worked extra shifts to pay tuition.

After her husband's death, Nichole continued going to therapy and focused on her mindset so that she could move forward. She wanted to take a good look at her life and discover what kind of person she wanted to be. At her core, she knew she was optimistic, and she enjoyed championing other people's goals and dreams.

Nichole's grief-related lack of appetite caused her to lose fifty pounds, and then she lost another forty pounds intentionally because she decided that being healthier was part of moving forward. Each class she took and pound she lost helped her feel more motivated and confident.

During that time, the extra hours she worked while finishing school showed her bosses her resilience, work ethic, and dedication to the company; they promoted her to manager at the lab. Then a year after her husband passed, she met a wonderful, caring man who is now her fiancé.

Although the untimely death of her husband was the source of great unhappiness, Nichole decided to make the experience a pivot point. Over the course of three years, she implemented changes that have made her healthier and happier.

Nichole says, "I wasn't as happy before my husband's death. I expected bigger things. And I expected more out of life and other people. After my husband passed, I realized that happiness comes from me. Happiness doesn't come from other people. If I have an optimistic, positive attitude toward life, and if I appreciate the little things that people do for me, then I will be a lot happier than waiting for things that may never come."

One evening when she came home from a stressful day at work and saw that her fiancé had taken the garbage and recycling out to the curb, she was thrilled. "I started tearing up," Nichole said. "I felt so happy and grateful that he took that one burden off my shoulders without me asking. I know it sounds silly, yet I'm learning to appreciate more and more little things like that instead of expecting big, grandiose gestures."

Nichole decided to manage one of the most devastating Happiness Zappers—the loss of a loved one—to make herself a happier person. And she did it one step at a time, initially by acknowledging the shock and pain from her grief. As she became ready, she took small steps to make changes that resulted in her feeling good. And now she's happier than she has ever been.

At some point, we all experience something that makes us unhappy—something that breaks our heart or a change that tests the essence of our being. We'll be forced to find a new normal because the past normal isn't an option. However, what that new normal feels like is based in large part on the choices we make and actions we take. We have to decide whether we want to live in the present and move forward or stay stuck in the memories of our past.

Kelliann experienced a mother's unfathomable nightmare. She was born in Michigan but moved to Cozumel with her mom after her parents divorced when she was a child. She met a man in Mexico whom she married when she was seventeen years old. Eventually they moved to the United States when she was twenty-four. By that time, she was a mother to three boys.

Shortly after she married, her husband became physically and emotionally abusive, and she often feared that he'd kill her. After fifteen years of an abusive marriage—where the majority of her focus had been on surviving—while living in El Paso and with the help of a good counselor, she found the courage to divorce him.

That year, her ex-husband picked up their three boys, ages eight, six, and four, for his Christmas visitation and didn't bring them back. For the next fifteen years, her sons lived with him as he moved around in Mexico. Although she tried to find them through relatives and the internet, she never came up with any viable leads.

"I don't like calling myself a victim," Kelliann said. "But in those days, that would have fit. The first decision I made was not killing myself." She believed that's exactly what her ex-husband wanted her to do. Then she thought, *Well, if I don't kill myself, but I become bitter, he wins, and he's not going to win.*

"When I look at the Society of Happy People's Types of Happiness, the one that's missing is stubborn happiness," Kelliann surmised. She decided, "I'm going to be happy because 'screw him.'"

Shortly after the kidnapping, Kelliann moved to Pennsylvania for a new job. Her friends in El Paso knew where she was and could find her in case her ex-husband or the kids came back.

Every morning, she'd think of things she used to like doing, things that made her feel good. She enjoyed growing plants, so she started doing that again. There was a soap opera she liked when she lived in Mexico that was now playing in the States, so she recorded it. By going back to what she once enjoyed, she slowly started putting herself back together with the goal to become happy again.

After this traumatic experience, she spent many years in therapy with more than one counselor. One of them told her that her sense of humor probably saved her life.

She got two master's degrees and wanted to study happiness. However, it was before Martin Seligman's positive psychology research was released, so most schools weren't offering happiness-focused degree plans.

She became professionally successful and now lives in Houston. Much of her happiness centers on noticing the small moments that help her feel good.

Fifteen years after the kidnapping, one of her sons came back to the United States, and they reunited. Over time, she also reunited with her other two sons. Now she knows they are alive and okay, which is an almost unexplainable type of relief. Her ex-husband died, so she feels that she'll never know the whole story about why he kidnapped their sons.

Kelliann still considers herself stubbornly happy because she's committed to being happy, no matter what life throws her way.

When she was younger, she felt that if something bad happened, it was going to last forever because she couldn't see the other side of it. She explained, "It's what happens when the fifteen-year-old has her heart broken for the first time. She feels she'll never fall in love again. However, by the time you get older, you realize that you can get through a lot.

"I'm actually grateful that a lot of people haven't had to go through as many things as I have," Kelliann said. "It's not a pleasant place to be. But when you get older, you realize when things are not good right now, they'll get better. Things always get better with time."

Kelliann feels that one of the best compliments people give her when they find out her story is "I never knew. You seem so normal." She lived through an unimaginably unhappy experience, yet she refused to let it define or change the essence of who she was. She was committed and determined to still feel happiness, to still feel good, to create a life that she wanted to live. She didn't deny her unhappy feelings but rather managed them with help so that she could live a happy life.

Unhappiness usually changes our life somehow. It can change the essence of who we are in an unhealthy way if we allow it. Or unhappiness can make us wiser, kinder, and more compassionate.

Sometimes unhappiness stretches over a long time. One unhappy experience after another adds up, and eventually they collectively change your life.

Grissette remembers a time when she went through a snowball of negativity over the course of several years that impacted her usually optimistic and positive thinking. Many unwanted changes had left her feeling weighed down by life. She had also reached a place where her expectations of what she thought her life should look like and what it did look like were different. That added pressure because she hadn't reached certain goals or milestones that she'd set in her mental timeline. Instead of living her dreams, she felt she'd gone through disappointments, setbacks, and frustrations, even though she realized she'd had some moments of happiness, too.

Those challenging years started with two miscarriages. She then moved from New York to Florida because of her fiancé's job. Although she looked for full-time employment, she didn't find it and had to do temp work. After two years, her fiancé's contract ended, and they moved back to New York, but it wasn't what she expected. Going back was different.

She took a temp job but within one month she knew. "This

job wasn't for me. There were so many red flags. Although my background was in HR, they offered me a full-time position in payroll. Since I hadn't had steady work for over two years, I felt like I needed to bite the bullet and accept it. It was the worst thing I ever did. I really should've listened to my gut and walked away, but I didn't."

At the time, Grissette had a casted broken foot and figured job hunting would be even more difficult, so she stayed at the payroll position. The workplace environment was extremely toxic, with bullying and demeaning conversations. The leadership kept implying they had done her a favor by hiring her and that she didn't appreciate it. Grissette didn't respond well to the negative, fear-based management style. She was always bumping heads with the bosses, and she was even timed when she went to the bathroom or spoke to someone in the hall.

This went on for fifteen months. Eventually, she requested two days off. Her boss didn't want her to take it, which led to a mutually agreed-upon layoff. She wasn't even upset when HR told her when her last day would be. Grissette explained, "I kept looking at it as the biggest blessing."

Her last day of work was February 13, and on February 25 she found out she had breast cancer. Her company insurance was ending February 28. Her first concern was figuring out her insurance and medical care options, but she still felt grateful she'd been laid off because she truly hated working in that toxic environment.

Even though Grissette had a solid support system of friends, family, and other cancer patients she met, she found herself in a negative state on a difficult journey. She was upset that chemo would cause her to lose her very long hair. "I cried almost uncontrollably for two weeks straight. Every time I thought of my hair, I bawled like a baby. *Oh my God, my hair, my hair.*"

Finally, Grissette thought to herself, *I can't avoid chemo. Well, what* can *I do?* Then she said, "You know what? I'm gonna shave my head because I don't want to see myself losing my hair."

She didn't have control of the cancer, but she felt that at least she had some control over her hair—one place where she could start feeling more positive. She wanted and needed to be in the best mental state possible.

"So, believe it or not, shaving my head was that first step. It was cliché and silly, but it's like the movies, like when they shave their head because they're getting ready for war. It literally felt that way. As silly as it sounds, shaving my head was kind of like getting ready for war. I was ready to fight the fight. I took what I was focusing on out of the equation."

Her treatments didn't go as well as she had hoped. She had an allergic reaction to the chemo. After the chemo, she had a lumpectomy, followed by radiation, and then maintenance infusions. She was part of the 1 percent of patients who have a reaction to the maintenance infusions, and she also ended up with cardiomyopathy.

When she was finally done with treatments, "I cried like a baby because I could not believe I was done after almost two years. It was an absolute happy cry, but I cried my butt off."

During those two years, she made an effort to be more positive. She joined a cancer group on Facebook that focused on humor. One of its members inspired her to start doing a positive Facebook post every morning and evening. Some days were harder than others. She still does these posts to start and end her day on a positive note, which has helped others stay positive, too. She was even invited to model in a cancer fundraiser and has been interviewed by an online publication.

Her grief had begun with her miscarriages. Then chemo closed the door on being able to have her own children. That was more grief she had to process, although she felt she had to get over it because she didn't really have a choice. She did let herself cry, cry, and cry some more.

Grissette also took a spiritual approach and realized, "Having kids is just not in the cards for me. I believe that our souls come back. At some point in another life, I'll come back and have my kids. Maybe not in this life but in the next one. Whatever you have to tell yourself that's going to make you take that next leap of faith into the next step, then you need to do it. That's what I did."

Despite the ups and downs of those years, she never regretted being laid off from the job that had made her miserable.

Sometimes unhappiness occurs in repeated waves that change what we thought our life would look like. When we experience unhappiness—even when it's hard and we're taking life one second, one minute, one hour, or one day at a time—we can also choose to recognize every moment when we feel good. We need to value these moments because they help us find a new normal that can be filled with happiness.

Unhappiness is part of life. It's an emotional experience that doesn't end on command because it's filled with many moving parts. Sometimes it takes a while for our physical reality and our emotions about it to align. Since life goes on, during our unhappy time we'll still experience other Happiness Zappers, too—some connected to our bigger unhappy experience, and others will be new.

Unhappiness usually involves grieving an aspect of life that we didn't want to end. And although our head knows that part of our life experiences will end within their natural course while others may cease early because of the unexpected, our heart takes a little longer to accept the reality. That's why we must respect the grieving process even when we don't enjoy it.

Maureen, a hospice chaplain, said that anticipatory grief can happen even before a loved one enters hospice. "They see their loved one's health failing," she explained. "They see that the doctors have fewer and fewer suggestions to prolong life. And you know, they finally get to a point of, 'Yeah, there's really nothing else we can do.' My chief role as a chaplain is just to listen. I hear a lot about what makes somebody sad, and what they are about to lose. It's a lot of unresolved emotions."

Everyone can experience anticipatory grief—and about more experiences than death. We can all start mourning what *might* happen if we lose our job, our health declines, or we think too far into the future.

A friend who was going through a really tough emotional time once told me, "It's just not worth being here. Ten years from now my dad will be dead, my dog will be dead, and my health will be worse because I'll be older. There's nothing to look forward to." I responded, "Well, there's a lot of living to do between now and ten years from now."

We can all anticipate and be consumed by the worst and unhappiest possibilities. But if we focus on the present moment instead, usually something is going on that can help us find a little bit of happiness.

We all know people who experience unhappiness. Maureen reminds us, "Sometimes just letting people pour out what's in their heart right then is all they need at the time. They need someone to listen and not try to fix it. I can't fix sadness. I can't fix loss. None of us can. And if we're suggesting how to fix it, it's what *we* would do for ourselves. It wouldn't necessarily work for someone else because they're not us. I read something about that: don't try to fix, don't try to solve things for people. If they're going through something and they've given you the honor of holding their story, just hold it and be. You can be empathetic, but don't try to fix it. They just want to know that somebody cares."

ZAP-MAP: Management Action Plan Tip

When we know someone who's unhappy, the best thing we can do is listen. When we're unhappy, the best thing we can do is find someone who'll listen to us.

When was a time that you felt better when you shared an unhappy experience but didn't receive advice?

When was a time that you only listened to someone who was in the middle of an unhappy experience without trying to fix it?

What other actions have you taken to manage unhappiness?

Stress

We all know how stress consumes us: Our body tenses up; our mind fills with paralyzing anxiety; emotionally we ping between flat, edgy, and everything in-between; and even our soul feels disconnected. Stress zaps our happiness by lowering our energy vibration, which makes everything feel stressful.

Elizabeth Scott, PhD, author of *8 Keys to Stress Management,* told me that one of the most common definitions of *stress* is "Anything that requires a response from us. The more the required response taxes us, the more depleted we feel from the stress.

"Then as we enter a stressful state, our focus narrows and we stop noticing opportunities that would either bring us happiness or provide support," she continued. "This is why excess stress is one of the most significant Happiness Zappers we have. Just as fear can quickly diminish any relaxation we might have as it puts us into 'survival mode,' stress can sap our joy as it puts us into a fight-or-flight response that narrows our focus and sucks the positivity right out of any experience."

Elizabeth shared how stress is an energy that even a baby can feel. She remembered taking her then-infant son shopping and told this story:

"We were having a wonderful day as he enjoyed all the new sights and sounds. He was all smiles until we went into a clothing store that had loud music and a sizeable crowd. As the music pulsed, he went from joyous to uncertain to decidedly irritable. As a growing crowd of strangers gathered around to smile and coo at him, his smile became strained and he started to cry. Joy became stress with too much intensity, and we had to leave the store until he got his bearings. When things quieted down, he was able to enjoy the day again, and we went back into a less crowded store."

Stress distracts us from enjoying life. When stress is environmental, like being around too many people in a noisy place, even a baby can feel stressed. We can all feel stressful energy. Have you ever walked into an office at work where two coworkers were engaged in a stressful conversation? You can feel the happiness-zapping energy. Some people may feel this more than others—they are often called *empaths*—yet everyone can feel it. Sometimes stress is literally in the air.

At other times our stress is created from specific situations. Robin worked at a job where her boss was her best friend. "We worked, did 5Ks, traveled, and played together," Robin said. "It was a great situation. We trusted each other. Then something happened, and all of a sudden, I didn't work there anymore. Not only did I lose my job, but I lost my best friend. I was really upset because I never really understood why. I had suspicions but never knew exactly what happened, so there wasn't any closure.

"It was stressful," she continued. "I couldn't get happy about any of it. I didn't have a job and needed to find one. Although I was job hunting, and had applied for what felt like a thousand jobs, I hadn't found one. I was struggling. Prior to my job ending, I'd won an all-expense-paid trip for two to Cancún from some work I'd done for the local chamber of commerce. However, I panicked thinking, *I can't go to Mexico because I don't have a job."*

Although Robin was more upset over losing her friend than the job, the whole experience added to the anxiety and depression that she dealt with daily. Her stressful circumstances zapped all the happiness out of what should have been a happy trip for her and her boyfriend.

Robin told me that her boyfriend convinced her to go by saying, "Robin, it's an all-expense-paid trip. You don't have to spend a dime. We need to go on this trip. You can worry about your job hunt when you get back. You're not losing anything."

When she landed in Cancún, she had a voicemail to schedule an interview for a job that she really wanted. She called and explained she was on a vacation and was told she could interview when she returned.

Robin said, "I almost let all of that negativity about losing my friend and job take away a fun and relaxing week in Cancún. Of course, finding out I got the interview after we landed helped me relax more. Then when I got back, I interviewed and got the job. I'm so glad that my boyfriend encouraged me to take that trip. If I'd missed that trip because of job hunting, I'd have been unhappy for a really long time."

The stressful, happiness-zapping time continued because Robin went through a series of job losses over the next few months before she landed her current job. Robin recently told her boyfriend, "This experience was meant to be. It took me a little while to get over the loss of my job and friend, then lose several other jobs. However, the right position eventually showed up for me. I'm so much happier in this job. I got two promotions in two years. My current job is way more fulfilling than I ever expected it to be. So, it all worked out."

Robin could have succumbed to the stress of an unexpected job hunt and the loss of an important friendship and skipped her trip. Yet she chose to manage these Happiness Zappers and allowed herself to take a much-needed trip with her boyfriend.

Sometimes stress sneaks up on us over time. Lupe worked for a large national sporting goods store for fourteen and a half years. She started in their management training program and within three months was a manager, in part because she's highly organized, paid attention to details, could fix problems, and was a quick learner.

She was so good at her job that she became the go-to person for the other managers and employees when they had problems to fix. She was even inundated with texts and phone calls when she was off work despite working, on average, fifty or more hours a week at the store.

"I'm a natural leader, coach, and mentor," Lupe explained. "It's rewarding when people count on you, and you can help the customers and your coworkers. I even felt proud that I could be helpful. However, eventually it felt like others were not doing their jobs because they could come to me. I was being taken advantage of and started feeling overwhelmed and underappreciated. Finally, I burned out. It became too stressful.

"Although I understand the need for companies to make changes, the last straw for me was when at the last minute they changed their vacation policy and I couldn't take my already scheduled vacation prior to the Thanksgiving holiday," she continued. "I gave my notice, and my last day was December 15."

It took Lupe about two months of resting and doing fun holiday things with her family, which she usually missed since she worked retail during the holidays, before she felt like starting her next job search.

Although she tried a few different career options, she's now working at an upscale retail store but has opted out of management for now. "Although I still find myself helping other employees and coaching them," she said, "at the end of most days I get to leave work at work. The pressure and stress of others not doing their jobs isn't on me anymore."

We often connect burnout to work, but it happens in other areas of our life too. It can happen when relationships are in a stressful state, when you're caretaking kids or someone who's ill, and even when you're doing something you want to do. At some point, everyone experiences the stress from feeling burned out from something.

Stress can be a prolonged experience—including unexpected job hunting because we were displaced, feeling burned out, dealing with health challenges for ourselves or people we love, or when our relationships with friends or family are going through a complicated time. Sometimes we have to coexist with the unknown—like a global pandemic, a war, political upheaval, loneliness, or other situations when life drastically and quickly changes.

Stress also comes from temporary, positive experiences, such as planning a wedding, vacation, or family holiday events. It also comes from when unplanned things, accidents, or annoyances happen. Managing the usual or unusual ups and downs of life can also be stressful.

There's even good stress. As Dr. Scott explains, "*Eustress* is good stress. It refers to the stress that keeps us challenged, on our toes, feeling vital and alive. With too little of this type of stress, we can feel bored and even depressed. However, even too much eustress can be a cause of distress and we feel overwhelmed and unable to meet the demands of a situation. Constantly taking on new tasks, making big decisions, and experiencing nonstop excitement can lead to burnout if it feels out of balance."

No matter the type of stress we experience, we have to manage it or the stress manages us. We need to be aware of when we are stressed because stress affects our physical, mental, and emotional health.

What are three stressful experiences in your life right now that zap your happiness? Are they controllable, uncontrollable, or a bit of both? Is it bad or good stress?

Stressor	Is it Controllable, Uncontrollable, or Both?	Is it Bad or Good Stress?

ZAP-MAP: Management Action Plan Tips

There are so many ways to manage your stress, but your way is unique to you. What works for one person or situation might not work for another. Here are a few common stress management tools:

- Acupuncture
- Cry
- Essential oils or scented candles
- Exercise
- Laugh
- Massage
- Meditation
- Music
- Play
- Read or listen to something motivational or inspirational
- Therapist or life coach
- Yoga

Fear

We're born with a hardwired fear sensor that helped us physically survive our caveman times by identifying mostly physical dangers so that we'd stay alive.

Fortunately, most of us aren't in that type of physical survival mode on a daily basis anymore. Most of us have enough food. We also have a place to live so that big critters can't eat us and we can protect ourselves (or evacuate) from extreme weather. However, some people's lives are threatened because of domestic violence, random gun violence, violent crimes, minority group profiling, famine, and war. Occasionally, severe weather is life-threatening. Accidents happen. Health challenges happen. Yes, some of our fears are real and need to be taken seriously because the worst *can* happen.

Everyone experiences fear that lurks in our minds and zaps our happiness: for example, fears of making and regretting a wrong decision, the unknown, not being in control, being emotionally hurt, failure, not being enough, or what others think, and so forth

"When I find myself feeling fearful for no real reason," Anna said, "I apply a commonly used 12-step program acronym to the situation: **F**alse **E**vidence **A**ppearing **R**eal. For example, when I feel fearful about how people may perceive me or other fears, I've retrained my brain. I remind myself that it's not real. And then, I'm all about taking little steps, putting one foot in front of the other to move forward and not get stuck in fear."

Allyson Chavez, a prosperity and transformational coach, shares that her favorite definition of *fear* is "the anticipation of pain." "We mostly try to deal with fear by denying it. Or we future-trip by living in the future, trying to figure out how we're going to handle an imaginary challenge that feels very real to us. We're not designed to do that." Allyson acknowledges that she mostly lived in fear for many years.

What helped Allyson work through the fear was to go to its opposite: faith. Allyson said, "Faith is truth spoken in advance.

So if fear is the anticipation of pain, then what does faith get to be the anticipation of? Can faith be the anticipation of relief? Can it be the anticipation of hope, or deliverance, or miracles, or joy, or whatever that word is, that really resonates with you? Then that's what you need to focus on."

She also asks herself, "*What's working for me right now?* Because the fear is that everything's going to fall apart? We're going to be in pain. We're going to be suffering. We're going have a loss and feel misery because we aren't feeling supported by God or the Universe. I ask, *What's working for me right now? How can I see that I'm supported, and everything always works out for me?*

"Several years ago, we were in dire financial straits and knocking on the door of bankruptcy. I was finally owning the power of my mind to really create the destiny and the reality that I desired. I remember going after a goal, and my first thoughts were *What if you don't get it?* and *What if none of this works?* That's actually the program I'd been running for years. There was lots of grinding, there was lots of sweat, there was lots of blood and tears and toil and pushing that eventually led to the bankruptcy. And when I saw what I was getting out of that, and that those thoughts still kept coming, that fear, *What if this doesn't work out?* I started telling myself, *Well, if this doesn't work out, then something else even better will come along.* If faith is my anticipation of deliverance and my anticipation of relief, or whatever word applies to me feeling better, then I just focused on that. If everything always works out for me, even if *this* doesn't work, then something better will come that will be even more magnificent and cause even greater happiness inside me. And that really helped to just calm the fear."

Even though Allyson's fear of filing bankruptcy became a reality, in hindsight because of her faith that everything works out for her, it ultimately became a lesson that helped her create her dreams.

Managing our fears starts with managing our mindset and how we think about the situations that trigger our fears. Then we need to follow up our mindset changes with new actions.

Leslee said, "For me fear isn't so much about something that might happen, like the roof is going to cave in or I'm going to get struck by lightning. It's the fear of the unknown, and sometimes that fear would paralyze me to where I would not try new things."

When Leslee went through her divorce, after a twenty-five-year marriage, she was committed to finding happiness again, to find herself again. "I had to learn how to get past that fear of new experiences," she said. "I started by asking myself, *What's the worst thing that could happen? Am I going to die?* No? Well, then just do it. Go try it. Go see if it's fun. See if it's beneficial. See if it makes you happy."

She always felt that as long as the leap wasn't something detrimental, such as losing your home or your job, she shouldn't be afraid to go on a trip by herself or talk to a stranger who might become a new best friend.

While she was going through her divorce, one of Leslee's close friends, who was very gregarious and liked to entertain, invited her to a party. This friend traveled all over the world and had friends from everywhere. This party was for one of her friends from France who was in town. Of the sixty people at the party, the hostess was the only person Leslee knew.

"Of course, the hostess didn't have time to talk to me and hold my hand the whole night," Leslee shared. "You know, she's the hostess, she's got to talk to everybody. So I started going up to people and talking to them. I met Anita from Puerto Rico. We've become great friends and even travel together. I also made some other friends from France and Morocco. That night I made four or five friends at that one party."

Leslee had to push herself to go to the party, yet pushing through that fear helped her grow. Now she's excited to go to parties because she never knows whom she'll meet. She learned that meeting people from new and different cultures makes her especially happy. She explained, "I like an international, eclectic circle of friends. It's fun to celebrate different holidays and learn new traditions."

It's natural for us to feel happiness-zapping fear from time to time, and obviously we need to determine if something is a real physical or emotional danger for us. If it is a real danger, we need to take the appropriate actions to stay safe. Sometimes the actions we need to take are preventative, such as going for our annual health checks, doing our car or home maintenance, paying attention when our intuition brings up a red flag about a situation or person, and keeping the lines of communication open with those we love. We can't stop every bad thing from happening. We can only make the best decisions about them with the information we have available to us.

We need to acknowledge our fears so that we can manage them. Otherwise, our fears manage us. Ultimately, we need to create a mindset that prompts us to take even small steps to move through our fears.

What are three fears that prevent you from taking action? Are they real, false evidence, or anticipation of pain?

Fear	Real? False Evidence? Or Anticipation of Pain?

ZAP-MAP: Management Action Plan Tips

If the fear is real and you're in physical danger, take the appropriate actions for your specific situation.

If the fear is mindset-based, identify it. Then figure out the small steps you can take to start moving through your fears. Some examples:

- Start looking for jobs you might like to apply for.
- Talk to a stranger at a party.
- Learn something new to build your confidence.
- Have a difficult conversation with someone to clear the air.
- Write down the things that are going right for you even if they seem small.

When you begin managing your fears, be compassionate with yourself. It takes time to reprogram how you think about something that has caused fear. You may even find it helpful to work with a life coach or therapist to learn the best way to manage your fears.

Chaos

Many situations cause us to feel like our circumstances are in disarray, unorganized, confusing, or chaotic. They usually happen unexpectedly, and the actual chaotic part of the experience is short-term. However, the aftermath can last longer.

We've all experienced common chaos:

- We overslept.
- Our boss has a critical project that takes precedence over the tasks we'd planned to complete when we arrived at work.
- A friend had a car accident and we need to pick them up.
- A tornado plowed through our neighborhood.
- Our child forgot to tell us about a school project until bedtime.
- Moving day.
- We're doing last-minute prep for a party, event, or trip.

Chaos often requires us to readjust our plans and priorities quickly because handling what's happening at that moment becomes the new priority.

Several years ago, Dallas experienced a rare long-term freeze. The news had reported that water pipes were bursting when the temperatures got warmer and everything started to thaw out. One morning, when I was walking downstairs from my third-floor bedroom, I heard running water. Initially, I thought I must have accidentally left my water faucet running in the kitchen.

When my feet hit the second floor, the water was louder, and I knew it wasn't from my sink faucet. A flooded room flashed in my mind as I continued quickly down the stairs to the first floor. My mind froze when I saw the floor flooded with more than a foot of water. I was in shock when I stood on a step above my water-filled office. The only thing that popped into my mind was, *Open the door to the garage*. I did, and it was also flooded. Then I opened the garage door so that the water from my first floor and the garage could exit onto the street.

I immediately started calling my neighbors for help, the city to turn off my water, and a friend to go to the store to get me some rain boots. It was chaotic for the next few hours: getting the water out of my townhouse, sorting the drenched items on the driveway where I put them to dry, and getting a crew in to remove the walls to prevent mold.

It took months to deal with the structural repairs and replace all my ruined stuff, yet the actual chaos only lasted a few hours while I was dealing with the initial logistics. Then the experience transitioned into other types of Happiness Zappers.

Despite the chaos, happiness still happened. Friends and neighbors helped me with the initial chaotic situation. Things could have been worse. Some of my neighbors had pipes burst on all three floors. I had insurance. I felt blessed despite feeling the chaos, too.

However, chaos isn't necessarily a Happiness Zapper for everyone. People who thrive in it are often called "adrenaline junkies." Some people—including EMTs and those in emergency services, fire departments, police departments, and hospital emergency rooms—are really chaos managers. Other professionals also deal with chaos, including IT departments when servers are down, power technicians when neighborhoods lose electricity, and organizations such as World Central Kitchen that go into disaster areas to feed people. Even some good experiences can involve moments of chaos, including having a baby, traveling on a vacation, job changes, moving, and hosting a party.

Shalisa, a manager at an upscale department store, reports, "I thrive in chaos. When I walk into work, if there are a lot of things thrown at me, I feel like it speeds me up to get those things done versus not having a lot to do. When it's chaotic, I manage my time differently. If I arrive at work and a few people have called in sick, I get a resignation notice, there are customer issues that need my attention, and we have lots of customers at the same time, it keeps me on my toes. Then, if you throw in a call from my son's school, it really forces me to balance everything and prioritize what gets done. I seem to get more done when there's a little chaos going on and I'm on a deadline."

When you thrive in chaos, you still have some stress, even if it's the good eustress.

What are the three most recent chaotic experiences that have affected you? How long did the actual chaos last? Was the chaos a Happiness Zapper, or did you thrive in it?

Chaotic Experience	How Long Did It Last?	Was It a Happiness Zapper, or Did You Thrive?

ZAP-MAP: Management Action Plan Tip

When you are in a moment of chaos, the first thing to remember is that it's short-term, so it either temporarily zaps your happiness or energizes you.

Sometimes, an experience lasts for a specific time, like if your neighbor has an emergency and asks you to keep her kids for a few hours. At other times, you may have additional details to deal with after the chaotic moments, but those things usually involve creating a longer-term plan.

Chaos, even the kind that you thrive in, can cause us to feel stressed, so some of those Management Action Plan Tips for stress can help here, too.

Annoyances

Annoyances are situations involving people or circumstances that can alter our mood but don't significantly change our lives other than zapping our happiness. Annoyances are highly personal. What annoys you may not annoy someone else. What bothers you on a specific day or at a certain time may not annoy you some other time. Annoyances are often really about our bandwidth. When we're feeling mostly happy and not stressed, we aren't as easily annoyed.

Tom said that when he was younger, things annoyed him a lot more. One of the big things that annoyed him was waiting in line. He said, "If I pulled up to a store and I realized it was gonna be a long line, I would drive fifteen minutes to go to find a shorter line, even if that took me a lot longer. I was a very aggressive, fast-paced type of individual. So if anything slowed me down from what I wanted to get done, it could be a problem. I'm still not where I want to be, but now I'm able to slow down if I'm in a line for ten minutes at Starbucks. It doesn't bother me at all. I've gotten better over time with that."

An annoyance can be something really minor, yet if we react to it, then we've given the power to zap our happiness to something that really doesn't matter.

Martha remembers being in a meeting with someone who swore a lot. "Initially, I thought, *That's really rude,*" she said. "I didn't say anything to him, but somebody else did. And then as time went on, I thought, *Well, he wasn't in a job interview with me. So what do I care what he says? Because it's none of my business. Why do I find that rude or insulting? He wasn't even addressing me in any way. He wasn't swearing at me. He was just talking.* It helped me realize that sometimes I get offended about things that are none of my business. You know, unless I see actual harm to someone or something, then I really need to keep my mouth shut because it's just an annoyance."

Often, our annoyances are from things that other people do that don't involve or impact us. If that happens, ask yourself, *Why does this annoy me?* You'll be a lot happier if you let it go, unless someone is being hurt.

Francisco, who lives in Spain, has a process he uses when assessing his Happiness Zappers. He starts by asking himself, *If that happens, what then?* And he keeps asking, *What then, what then, what next?* until he gets a final answer.

He shared how this worked for him: "I had a very unexpected tax bill. I was, like, 'This is not right,' so I started looking into it. It turned out that even though it wasn't right, I was probably gonna have to pay it anyway. My first reaction was to be very upset and frustrated about it. But then I took the next step and said, *Okay, so what if I have to pay this? What happens next?* So I have to do this and that to pay the bill. Then I asked, *So, what's the actual consequence?* And it turns out that the actual consequence is more about me being annoyed than the actual money I had to pay. It's not gonna change my life in any way or have any objective impact on it."

If Francisco hadn't taken himself to the final step, he would have been stuck being annoyed and having his happiness zapped. Instead, he came to the conclusion, "It's annoying, but there's nothing I can do about it, so I might as well not spend any time thinking about it." When he follows this process, it helps him create a more relaxed frame of mind and reduces his stress, so it makes managing Happiness Zappers easier.

How we manage our Happiness Zappers, even the largely insignificant ones like annoyances, determines how long they are able to do their zapping. Sometimes understanding the worst thing that can happen might be the easiest way to create the best plan to manage it.

List your last three annoyances and how long you'll remember each of them.

Annoyance	How Long Will You Remember It?

ZAP-MAP: Management Action Plan Tip

If you won't remember it a year from now, let it go.

CREATE YOUR PERSONAL ZAPPER MANAGEMENT ACTION PLANS (ZAP-MAPS)

Now that you've identified some of your Happiness Zappers, it's time to create your own ZAP-MAP: Zapper Management Action Plan. Whenever you feel that a Happiness Zapper is zapping too much of your happiness, change how you think about it so that you can take steps to manage it. Otherwise, the Happiness Zapper manages you.

Since most of our Happiness Zappers are unique to us, how we manage them is also unique to us. Each person handles differently the biggies like grief, unexpected job loss, or health challenges. Since each person's Happiness Zappers are different, and can even change day-to-day, how we manage them changes, too. Happiness Zapper management is always customized to you and your ever-changing situations, so stay flexible.

Creating a Zapper-Management Action Plan (ZAP-MAP) is quick and easy, with four simple steps that you've already started:

1. Identify the Happiness Zapper.
2. Specify the type of zapper: unhappiness, stress, fear, chaos, or annoyances.

3. Decide if the zapper is controllable, uncontrollable, or a bit of both.
4. Determine actions you can take to manage the zapper.

Your ZAP-MAP will look similar to this:

Happiness Zapper	Type of Happiness Zapper	Is it Controllable, Uncontrollable, or Bit of Both	Zapper Management Action Plan
Social Media Bums Me Out	Annoyance	Controllable	• Limit the amount of time I'm on Social Media • Dig deep to figure out why it pushes my emotional buttons
Rush Hour Traffic	Stress	Bit of Both	• I can't control the actual traffic • I can control the time I leave and what I do when I'm driving— like listening to inspirational books or music or enjoy the silence
Family Pet Died	Unhappiness	Uncontrollable	• I have to let myself grieve so it's okay, to feel sad and cry • Recognize grief is a process that I walk through at my own pace • Seek professional help if needed

ZAP-MAP Step One: Identify the Happiness Zapper

Review the exercises in the previous sections to identify some of your current Happiness Zappers, or you can identify new ones. Pick the experiences that zap your happiness most often.

ZAP-MAP Step Two: Specify the Type of Zapper

Once you identify some of the experiences that zap your happiness, determine which type of Happiness Zapper each experience is: unhappiness, stress, fear, chaos, or annoyances. Some zappers may be more than one type, but focus on the type that's dominant.

ZAP-MAP Step Three: Decide If the Zapper Is Controllable, Uncontrollable, or a Bit of Both

The one thing we can *always* control is our reaction to a situation. That doesn't mean denying how we feel about it or pretending it's positive if it's not; it simply means not impulsively reacting badly to those feelings. For example, if someone says something hurtful to you, you don't have to respond the same way at that moment. Take some time to think through your response.

We have no control over some situations: the weather, if your company is doing displacements, what people think or say about you, or if your internet goes down.

We have control over other situations: what we eat, whether we exercise, with whom and how we spend our time. We decide if we're going to learn something new, meet new people, or visit a new place.

We can't control if we're diagnosed with high blood pressure, but we can control how we treat it. We can't control if a blizzard is coming, but we can control how we prepare for it. We can't control another person's reaction to us, but we can control our communication and actions toward them.

Michelle Wax, who started the American Happiness Project, told me, "I really work hard to be as calm as possible. It helps to acknowledge if something is in my control or not. If it's not, I tend to let it go. Something very recent that was causing stress was the *American Happiness Documentary* premiere. I was stressed that there'd be some technical internet glitch. I had all these people watching and wanted it to be professional and go smoothly. When I got stressed thinking about it, I asked myself, *Is this within my control?* I know I can't control if the internet randomly goes out, so I just released it, saying, 'It's going to be okay. People will understand if something happens.' That's what I do. I acknowledge my feelings, which brings them to the surface so that I'm self-aware of them—and then control what I can, and let go of the rest because that's the best I can do."

Acknowledging what we can or cannot control helps us know what we should focus on and what we should leave aside. When the only thing we can control is creating a contingency plan for the possibility that the worst happens, after we've done that, we need to let it go and instead focus on what's going right.

ZAP-MAP Step Four: Determine Actions You Can Take to Manage the Zapper

Once you've identified your Happiness Zappers, the type of zapper, and whether it's in your control, you can make your ZAP-MAP. This ZAP-MAP is customized for you and your specific Happiness Zapper, and it needs to be flexible. How you manage your Happiness Zapper(s) is based on changing circumstances and current situations.

When other people are part of our Happiness Zappers, remember that most of the time, they are trying to get their needs or wants met and really aren't thinking about your needs or wants. Therefore, when we create our ZAP-MAPs that involve other people, we need to question our motives for our actions toward them. Are we seeking a reaction or a solution that works for all parties involved? Sometimes our actions, which include what we say, are really an attempt to manipulate how someone responds to us so that we get what we want. Instead, an effective plan that involves other people is about trying to find a solution that best meets everyone's needs.

One of the most challenging parts of managing our Happiness Zappers is determining when we should take action and when we need to be patient. Rainer Maria Rilke suggests, "Live the questions now." If our ZAP-MAP doesn't feel good or reveal itself relatively easily, then try to sit in the question and let the plan come together. Rarely, if ever, does being reactionary make us happier.

Below are some tools that can be part of your ZAP-MAP and help you better manage your Happiness Zappers. The most important ZAP-MAP tool is your mindset management because that determines your focus.

ZAP-MAP TOOLS

Mindset

Two of my favorite quotes about mindset come from James Allen, author of the bestselling classic (1903) *As a Man Thinketh*:

"Men do not attract which they want, but that which they are."

"As he thinks, so he is; as he continues to think so he remains."

These quotes remind us that if we want to experience more happiness, or anything else, we must have the correct mindset.

That doesn't mean ignoring when we feel bad because of an experience. When we do that, our bad feelings simply fester and get bigger. *It does mean choosing to not let our Happiness Zapper experiences define us* to the point where we get stuck reliving them over and over again in our minds. When we do this, we aren't living in the present and we aren't moving forward. Instead, we are chained to the past and attracting more unhappy experiences.

Therefore, the most important tools we have to manage any of our Happiness Zappers are our mind and how we think. We need to ask ourselves what's going right in the moment, even if it's just the small things that make us feel a little better. If the moment made us feel better, we need to cherish and value it. Looking for these moments needs to be the foundation of our mindset.

The mindset theory is easy, but like all things, the application can be more of a challenge. Be kind to yourself if you can't maintain your positive mindset all the time. None of us can. Sometimes, having a short pity party is okay. However, the operative word is *short*.

Notice even the smallest moments of happiness. This allows you to create a happy mindset habit by recognizing what makes you feel better, good, and happier.

Other tools you can use to create your ZAP-MAP include:

Acceptance

The Serenity Prayer asks for the "courage to accept the things we cannot change." Acceptance of situations that we can't change is often the most challenging part of managing some Happiness Zappers. When we deny something we can't accept, the situation manages us.

Ganesh shared that when he and his wife found out their daughter was autistic, they didn't know what to expect. "It was chaotic and a little bit fearful," he said. "Then, five years later, I read an article that precisely articulated this experience. It was about *That Child Syndrome.* So basically, if you have a child who dies, even though that's tragic, there's closure. However, when you have an autistic child, you're expecting this wonderful, beautiful child. And yes, the child is wonderful and beautiful when it's born, as you expected. It does everything for the first six months, and maybe a year, and then it slowly starts to show regression. Now what you have is a mental memory of the child, and the reality is very different. You're not able to let go of that mental memory, and then you have to reconcile with the physical person in front of you. That was very painful. And it took us about five years to get through that. It was a very difficult time because we didn't understand what we were going through. After the fact, when I came across this article it made sense. I think once you get closure, which in some cases is acceptance, then you're able to let go of your expectation and deal with the reality. In our case, it's loving our beautiful daughter for who she is."

It can be difficult to accept situations we can't control. When this happens, it zaps our happiness. Once we've accepted a situation and stop tainting it with our own desires and expectations, we can find peace because that situation no longer manages us.

Boundaries

We all need to know and set our limits. Without boundaries, our happiness is zapped by others. Brené Brown reminds us, "When we fail to set boundaries and hold people accountable, we feel used and mistreated."

We knowingly or unknowingly set boundaries in six areas:

- Physical
- Emotional
- Time
- Sexual
- Intellectual
- Material

Some boundaries are easy to set, but they may not always be easy to implement.

It's also relatively simple to set boundaries around people we don't know well. If a new neighbor moves next door and says something that makes us feel uncomfortable, it's pretty easy to ignore them. It's easy to not share much about our personal lives with coworkers or customers. It isn't difficult to have boundaries with people with whom we don't have an emotional connection.

Boundaries become harder and more challenging when we need to set them with people we care about, and sometimes those situations usually involve a wider circle of people. If you need to set boundaries with a sibling, your parents could be put in the middle. When you need to set boundaries with a child, it affects the entire family. Even boundaries with friends can be complicated if we are connected to other mutual friends. Setting boundaries with someone we date can be hard because we may hope the other person will change.

Once we set and implement boundaries, they help protect our happiness so that it's not being zapped as often—and you can reevaluate the boundaries you've set at any time and adjust them as needed.

Breathe

"When life gets chaotic, I always stop and breathe. That's the essence of life," shared Pheng, a driver with the car service I use, during one of our in-depth and thought-provoking conversations about life on our way to the airport one morning. While we all instinctively breathe, we don't always use our breath as a tool to help reset our bodies and minds when we feel the immediate effects of a Happiness Zapper.

When we start feeling anxious, stressed, or angry, we usually start taking short, shallow breaths, which then intensify those feelings. Instead, we should pause; take a few deep, lung-filled breaths; and hold them for a few counts before exhaling so that we can reoxygenate. This step allows the mind and body to relax so that we can be more thoughtful about our reactions.

Breathing that heals can be done practically anywhere. Our breathing connects us to life, and by practicing conscious breathing, it literally helps us respond in a thoughtful and possibly divinely inspired manner.

Communication

Everyone knows the happiness-zapping experience of poor communication. Sometimes it's hard to express ourselves or to hear what someone else needs to say. So because communicating can be difficult, we're inclined to avoid it. But this only increases our Happiness Zapper experiences.

Chantal said that she avoids uncomfortable conversations especially at work. She ended up in a situation where a coworker kept getting or sharing credit for Chantal's work. Finally, after a national meeting where she was surprised when she and this coworker were recognized for a project that Chantal had done alone, she knew she had to address the situation with her boss or she'd stay angry. Also, her coworker wasn't correcting the misplaced credit, which made the situation even more uncomfortable.

Chantal was torn about discussing this with her boss because the coworker was also her friend. "However, when I spoke with my boss, I used an example that he'd given me," said Chantal. "He was in a situation where somebody else at the corporate office got credit for his work, and he was really annoyed about it. He'd mentioned it to me several times in the past, so I nicely brought up that situation and reminded him of how he felt. I then mentioned to him about a couple of examples when somebody else got credit for my work. I told him that it hurt my feelings, and I felt like I didn't get the recognition I deserved. I felt better after addressing the situation instead of continuing to ignore it. Since I did it in a way that he understood, he definitely got where I was coming from. It was a positive conversation."

Not all conversations like Chantal's are positive. She even acknowledged, "Sometimes when you bring up things like this with a boss, they may have a negative reaction to it because, like in this case, my boss should have known that it was my work.

And he should have made that correction, so it's kind of like he dropped the ball with our corporate office."

Effective communication can be difficult, and when we need to have a difficult conversation to manage one of our Happiness Zappers, it's best if we take a little time to think it through instead of reacting to the first thoughts that pop into our head. We also need to accept that communication requires all parties involved to participate in a constructive manner, and sometimes that's not possible. At that point we may need to set boundaries to manage a happiness-zapping relationship.

Decisions

The fear of making a wrong decision often puts us in a state of paralysis by analysis. We stay stuck and do nothing. Some decisions are easily made, where it's obvious what is right or wrong. Usually, if we follow the Golden Rule of treating others as we'd want to be treated, it helps take some indecision out of the equation.

But some decisions create stress and zap our happiness because the decision isn't about right or wrong but would simply lead to different outcomes:

- Do I apply for a promotion?
- Do I go on this vacation?
- Do I enroll in this class?

- Do I attend this party?
- Do I communicate about a difficult situation with someone I love?
- Do I change my lifestyle to be healthier?
- Do I set a boundary with someone?
- Do I try something new?
- Do I buy a new car?

No decision can guarantee an absence of all Happiness Zappers. Different choices bring different zappers, and how we manage them determines our happiness.

Forgiveness

When someone has harmed us, it's often difficult to let those experiences go. It's easier to stay rooted in our right to be angry or hurt, but all those emotions tie us to the past. Forgiveness doesn't mean forgetting that someone hurt you. It doesn't mean seeing someone who hurt you again. Forgiveness does mean that a person or past incident doesn't control your emotions and actions anymore. It means you get to experience peace and are no longer tethered to the past, so you can move forward and enjoy the present.

Sometimes the person we need to forgive is ourselves. We all make mistakes, and sometimes forgiving ourselves makes it easier to forgive others.

Forgiveness can take time, yet once we've forgiven someone, it reduces the power of that person or situation to zap our happiness. Instead, the experience simply becomes a lesson learned.

HALT

One of the lessons in 12-step programs is HALT. It reminds people to never let themselves get

- Hungry
- Angry
- Lonely
- Tired

If you want to manage your Happiness Zappers well, you can't be in one of these states. Each one can zap your happiness. They create low energy, and you'll make your decisions from a place of neediness instead of what you want to experience or create.

When you feel your happiness has been zapped, see if you're in the middle of a HALT experience. If you are, address that first so that you can move forward effectively.

Movement

Steve Jobs, Aristotle, and Charles Dickens were all known for holding walking meetings.

Why did they do so? Because moving your body helps you de-stress, feel more energetic, increase productivity, and inspire creativity.

Any body movement shifts and increases your energy, which helps you manage unhappiness, stress, fear, chaos, and annoyances. Movement also activates all your feel-good body chemicals. Movement can be anything from a robust physical workout to something that is more about flow—like a walk, tai chi, or even sex. Picking an activity that makes you feel good transforms your energy and, therefore, how you feel.

"Dancing puts me in a joyful mood," Maureen shared. "Even if I've been dealing with cranky customers at work or other challenging situations, listening to the music and dancing just make me feel better."

Pause

We can instantly communicate, even when we aren't doing it in person. That's convenient, but it also adds complications because we can easily respond to someone's comments or actions *in real emotional time* before we've had a chance to process our feelings about what they said or did. It's too easy to text, send an instant message, comment on social media, or email something that we might not say in person.

There are times when we have to set boundaries or say things that might hurt someone's feelings in order to take care of ourselves.

If you feel stressed, angry, tired, or confused, consciously choose to pause before you do or say something that can't be undone or unsaid. Give yourself a little time and space to process your feelings, and then resolve your situation in a positive manner rather than simply emotionally reacting to it. You'll often discover that saying or doing less yields the best results for everyone.

Reframe

We all get to choose how we view an experience. Even unhappy experiences can teach us something when we look for the lessons that can make our lives better instead of getting stuck in the pain. We can quickly reframe how we perceive many little experiences that zap our happiness.

Vickie said she doesn't have a lot of Happiness Zappers in part because she tries not to be around negative people. However, sometimes in public she finds herself around others who are rude. To manage this annoyance, she's decided to give these people the benefit of the doubt by reframing how she sees them. Instead of thinking they are being rude for the sake of being rude, Vickie explained, "I think if someone is rude, they're probably going through stress that they are not able to handle, so they're lashing out at the first person who comes around—and sometimes that happens to be me. I also try not to take things personally because I don't think most people really mean it when they're rude."

Vickie's reframing reminds me of when I started taking the same approach. I know I looked run-down and haggard when I arrived at the airport. It would be a natural assumption if everyone thought I was going on a much-needed vacation for the Labor Day weekend. Nothing could have been further from the truth. My mom had been in the ICU on a respirator for almost three weeks. We'd decided it was time to remove it the following morning. However, there is absolutely no way anyone on that plane could have known that the next day was going to be the worst day of my life. After that, I stopped judging how other people, especially strangers, act. I understood then, with every fiber of my being, that I had no idea what was going on with them, and their truth could be just as devastating as mine.

Karen Haller, author of *The Little Book of Color* and a global speaker on color psychology, told me, "I see every negative comment about my book or a lecture as a piece of gold. I reframe it. I don't need to talk to the people who already love color. I need to talk to all the people who think color is one load of rubbish. That's what fascinates me: Why does someone think of as rubbish something that is so innate, so important, and such an integral part of our life, and such an emotional hook that brings so much joy to many? That's the question I want to be able to answer. And for everyone who says something negative, I stop and go, 'Thank you so much for saying that. I'm fascinated why you think that. I want to understand how you're thinking and what's going on.' Because that's research. It's absolute gold."

Many experts don't take criticism of their work as well as Karen does. Karen has reframed what some might see as a negative and instead uses it to make her a better teacher so that she can better explain a subject she loves.

Reframing allows us to glean something positive from happiness-zapping situations. It gives us a choice to feel good by seeing the best, even when we experience Happiness Zappers.

Smile

Seth Godwin once shared that a sales director at a large New York organization hired a theater director to teach his sales team to smile. Sales went up 15 percent within three months of the lessons.

Smiles are a powerful form of communication, and many scientific studies prove how smiling benefits us:

- Even fake smiles activate feel-good endorphins.
- Smiling is contagious.
- People who smile are perceived as cooler.
- Smiling reduces pain.
- People who smile at work are more likely to receive promotions and earn higher incomes.
- People who smile are perceived as better looking.

Like breathing, smiling is something that you can do in almost any situation to change your vibe and energy. Sometimes, your smile might even help the other people you are interacting with during that moment.

Venting

Sometimes we need to vent about our Happiness Zappers so that we can process and release those thoughts and feelings. However, healthy venting requires us to only vent to people who won't add to the negative energy around the experience. A simple way to test this is to ask yourself, *When I'm talking to whomever, does their feedback add to my anger, angst, and anxiety about the situation?* If the answer is yes, don't vent to that person. Also ask yourself, *Is it someone who will keep our conversation private?* If the answer is no, don't vent to that person.

Ferrell shared how she learned about healthy venting: "My mother was very, very good at this. When she found herself feeling overwhelmed, upset, angry, annoyed, or whatever, she'd call me and say, 'I need a ten-minute pity party.' I'd say okay, and I'd sit there, and she would rant and rave, talk and cry, whatever she needed to do. Then I'd hear a timer go off in the background and she'd say, 'Okay, time to change the subject. Let's talk about something happier.' Then we'd spend the next however long just talking about the good things that were happening. Since she acknowledged her feelings in a safe environment, she was then able to let it go so that she could move on. Usually during our conversation, we were able to come up with either a solution to whatever the problem was, or she'd say, 'Okay, I realized that's not important. I can let it go.'"

Ferrell carries on her mom's tradition by using the ten-minute pity party to manage her Happiness Zappers.

Managing your Happiness Zappers is personal. There is no one-size-fits-all formula because each Happiness Zapper is unique to you. However, they are manageable when you follow this simple ZAP-MAP formula:

1. Identify the Happiness Zapper.
2. Specify the type of zapper: unhappiness, stress, fear, chaos, or annoyances.
3. Decide if the zapper is controllable, uncontrollable, or a bit of both.
4. Determine actions you can take to manage the zapper.

Happiness Zapper	Type of Happiness Zapper	Is it Controllable, Uncontrollable, or Bit of Both	Zapper Management Action Plan

Apryl shared, "I've known some profound unhappiness, and so I think that, in some ways, it just really motivated me even more to go the opposite direction. One of the most important lessons I learned is that I'm in control of my happiness. Some of the unhappiness I experienced or allowed myself to experience really was because I was placing my happiness in someone else's hands: either a significant other, a job, or my family. I also had some health issues. And I've experienced stress, fear, chaos, and annoyances. But every day I wake up with this idea that I get to decide about my happiness. It doesn't mean I'm smiling and laughing all the time, but I generally get to decide what the day looks like, what happiness looks like for me."

Managing Happiness Zappers isn't about eliminating them. Instead, it's about accepting—and even expecting—that sometimes our life isn't going exactly as we planned or hoped it would.

When we manage our Happiness Zappers, we get to decide if they are going to consume us or be fleeting moments in our day. We also make the decision about how much happiness we notice in spite of them.

Print off your ZAP-MAP at sohp.com/zm.

Principle Three: HAPPINESS CHANGES AS YOU CHANGE

When I worked for the Hazelden Foundation in the self-help field in the 1990s, one of my favorite parts of the job was planning events and selecting the guest speakers for them. One of the authors whom I had the pleasure of hosting was Karen Kaiser Clark. Her book *Life Is Change, Growth Is Optional* and signature speech altered how I thought about my life.

A couple of years after college, I transferred with my job to its West Palm Beach office. I'd always wanted to live in another state, and "Palm Beach" sounded glamorous. It was the first time I'd lived anywhere other than Abilene, Texas, and I didn't know what to expect, but I had big hopes and dreams for my new adventure.

However, the reality proved to be more challenging than glamorous. Almost from the day I arrived, my relationship with my new boss was difficult, and my big-to-me $5,000 raise didn't stretch as far as I thought it would. Money was tight, and I missed the familiarity of where I grew up—and my friends and family. Most days I thought I'd made the biggest mistake of my life. But I was full of youthful pride and determined to stick out my two-year commitment to my job, believing that things would change for the better. I also wanted to learn to love my new city, one I chose to live in, a change I chose to make.

It took a few years, but I made some great friends; got a roommate, which helped me save money; and realized I could always get a new job working for a boss who at least liked me. In hindsight I chose to make changes and grow. I chose to recognize the happiness in my experiences instead of looking for it in achieving a goal. But when Karen Kaiser Clark came to speak, I was still evaluating whether moving a few years earlier had been a wise decision.

Growth is rarely instantaneous. Often, growth is only recognized from the perspective of hindsight. Only then can we realize how one change influenced another, setting off a domino effect in our lives, and triggering the change, growth, and even happiness we failed to see when we were going through the actual experience.

On the surface, the concept of "Life Is Change, Growth Is Optional" feels obvious. Life changes. Sometimes those changes are wanted. Sometimes they aren't. Sometimes we choose or influence the changes. Other times they are thrust upon us. However, whatever the reason for change, our response determines if it is a catalyst for personal growth, stagnation, or even regression; likewise, this response also determines if the change increases or reduces our happiness or doesn't impact it at all.

Most of us know that our response to anything is what matters in most situations. However, how we respond isn't always about what our mind knows. Often how we feel about a situation influences our response more than our mind does. We often know something but don't act on it. For example, we know the foods we shouldn't eat because they make us feel bad or gain weight, yet we probably eat some of them anyway.

We instinctively resist change because it means different, new, and uncertain. Even *changes we want* can create anxiety or fear, alongside the butterflies of excitement.

If you went away to college, remember the day you arrived at your dorm? You were excited about your new adventure, being independent from your parents, and beginning your adult life. However, your stomach was also probably filled with butterflies. Some made you queasy because you wondered about the unknown. Others made you excited because you were ready to soar into your new future. That's the complexity of even wanted changes: they can be exhilarating and scary at the same time.

Other changes are more complicated. Sometimes there are different options, without a clear choice. You might get a surprise job offer at another company even though you're happy with your current job. Taking the new job or staying at the current one will affect your career path, yet neither choice is obviously right or wrong. They just provide different experiences.

Sometimes change is unintentional. You may not notice when it happens until time has passed and the aftereffect appears. Maybe you talked to a friend every day for years. Then, little by little, some of your common connectors change: where you work or live, or if one of you married or had kids. Gradually, your conversations went from daily to weekly, then to monthly, and then to every few months. One day, you realize that it's been years since you've spoken with this person who was once a part of your everyday life. Now, your only communication is the occasional like or comment on a social media post or text, which is vastly different than actual conversations. The change wasn't intentional. The person probably doesn't make you unhappy, but life changes altered your relationship.

Some changes are thrust upon us. Your company decides that you're the perfect person for a new job that you didn't even want, so all of a sudden you have new work responsibilities.

Someone in your family gets cancer, so everyone joins Team Survivor to help them get well. Or a hurricane devastates the community where you live, leaving you and your neighbors to rebuild homes, schools, and businesses.

To start thinking about how life changes, compare some of your past happy experiences with current ones:

Past Happiness	Current Happiness
Who was your best friend in fourth grade?	Who is your best friend now?
What was your favorite song in high school?	What is your favorite song now?
What was your favorite food as a child?	What is your favorite food now?
Where was your first job?	What is your career now?
What was your favorite social activity ten years ago?	What is your favorite social activity now?

Most likely, but not always, your past and current happiness answers are different. What made you happy changed because you or your life changed. Many things can contribute to these changes, but the most common ones are maturity, life changes, experiences, and the unexpected.

- **Maturity** comes from the natural process of growing older and the experiences that influence your mental and emotional behavior.
- **Life changes** are big events that alter your perspective and even your actual daily existence.
- **Experiences** provide you with knowledge and empathy as a result of what you do, see, and feel.
- **The unexpected** are those moments that show up in your life without warning or anticipation but can shift everything in an instant.

Wanted or unwanted, planned or unplanned, changes involve a new normal. Even when changes are wanted, they can still be uncomfortable. Many aren't desired, welcomed, or easy, yet our life will always be full of them. Although we can't control many changes, we can control our attitude about how we navigate them—which, of course, influences the happiness we find in them.

MATURITY

Age alone doesn't make us mature, although it does contribute to our maturity. Neuroscience now suggests that the human brain's ability to make decisions isn't fully developed until we're about twenty-five years old. However, the older we are, the more we've experienced and learned.

Our experiences give us the opportunity to gain wisdom. We either become wiser by learning from our past, or we stay stagnant by doing the same things over and over and getting the same results. Maturity comes when we've gained wisdom so that we can reflect and make different choices about future situations, especially if we didn't like how a past experience turned out.

Everyone has one or more of these stories, where you wished you'd been as wise and mature as you thought you were at the time. Here's one of mine. In the late 1980s, I had just graduated from college. I was twenty-one with big hair, oversized shoulder pads, and, to my mom's dismay, usually bright red lipstick. I'd recently landed my first professional job, moved into my first apartment, and believed, like most people that age, I knew almost everything.

After my parents divorced, my mother had moved about an hour away from me. She had a part-time job at the VFW

Hall on their bingo nights. One of the weekends I went to see her, it ended up being bingo night on the day I arrived. She wanted—expected—me to go with her.

"Why do I have to go?" I responded, with my eyes rolling as my tone quickly changed from pleasant to annoyed.

"Because my friends want to meet you," my mom replied.

But I was twenty-one and not thinking of her feelings. Instead, I cavalierly replied, "Why would they want to meet me? I'm sure we don't have anything in common."

My mom's voice escalated. "With that attitude, you probably don't. You're not better than they are."

"I didn't say I was," I yelled back. "I just don't want to go sit in a smoky room with old people."

"I can't believe you're such a snob," my mom replied on the verge of tears. "I didn't raise you to be that way."

I felt bad that I made her cry. I agreed to go with her for a while, but that didn't change my attitude. We've all had that moment: the crossroads where we could have made the right choice and created a wonderful memory, or where we made a wrong one and were left with regrettable ones. I was being a brat, and at least part of me knew it.

Even though I went with my mom as a result of her guilt trip and the accusation that I was being pretentious, I wasn't happy about it. Once there, I went through the paces of smiling and making small talk with her friends. I was polite—but not engaged and present. I counted down the minutes until I could leave instead of even trying to enjoy a game of bingo, meeting new people, and, most importantly, spending time with my mom.

Given the chance, I'd redo that night, and probably a few others, now that my mother's been gone since 2004. In hindsight, all my mom wanted to do was introduce to her friends the daughter she'd talked about and to show me off a little bit.

My more mature self would have happily said, "It'll be fun to spend time with you and your friends." I could have taken more allergy meds to counteract the smoke, had real conversations with the friends who adored her, and maybe sat at that bar, ordered a drink, and talked to the vets about their experiences. I'd embrace the opportunity to be with my mom and talk to people who had lived a history I'd only learned about in school.

But I was young and immature. I couldn't understand my mother's idea of a perfectly happy evening. If only I'd been as wise as I thought I was at that time. I was only thinking of the situation from my point of view, which also didn't grasp that one day my mom would be gone, along with opportunities like this one.

I don't remember when I started regretting that incident. I do know that at some point, probably a few years later, I started valuing the time I spent with her even if we weren't doing something that I wanted to do. I started to understand that just spending time with my mom was the happy moment in itself because being together is what mattered—and that's maturity.

Sometimes you mature naturally and get wiser. But many times, you gain real wisdom as a result of experiences, especially the ones where the lessons took a little time to understand.

Maturity isn't always related to age. It can also be emotionally based. We can find ourselves acting immature even when we are wise enough to know better. When our life is filled with Happiness Zappers, we become emotionally drained and reactive instead of thinking through our responses. We may find ourselves yelling at our kids, partners, or even a stranger trying to help us. Or our immature behavior may escalate beyond speaking our mind to doing things like smashing a tennis racket, drinking too much, or arguing with strangers on social media.

Since maturity, or the lack of it, is often recognized only in hindsight, think about a few situations where you may or may not have been as mature as you'd like to have been and what you learned from them.

When was a time in the past that you acted immature?
How old were you?
How did it make you feel?
Would you act the same way now?

When was a time recently that you wish you'd acted more mature after you lost your cool?
What was going on that zapped your happiness at that time?

When was a time that you wanted to react one way but *decided* to act maturely instead?
How old were you?
How did it make you feel?
Did you act mature as a result of a past experience when you reacted a different way?

In most situations, our maturity defines how we respond to our circumstances, and our response determines our happiness in that moment. As we mature, it changes our opportunities for happiness. Sometimes an unhappy experience helps us mature and influences our future responses to similar situations.

LIFE CHANGES

Some of our life changes happen over time, and others in a nanosecond.

Christopher Reeve, forever known as Superman, always pops

into my mind as someone who was forced to renegotiate happiness when his life changed instantly. For those who don't remember, Reeve was thrown from his horse during an equestrian competition, at the height of his acting career, becoming paralyzed from the shoulders down.

However great his acting accomplishments were, his legacy was defined by how he dealt with that tragic accident. He could have stayed stuck in grieving his old life: the one of a handsome, healthy, vibrant, successful actor.

Instead, Christopher embraced this new and difficult present. He set an example for others by keeping his body strong so that when better treatment options became available, he'd be ready for them.

He used his celebrity to bring more attention to spinal cord injuries and the people who suffered from them. He and his wife, Dana, founded the Christopher Reeve Foundation and lobbied on behalf of people with spinal cord injuries.

He allowed a life-changing moment to expand his purpose, becoming an activist and inspiration to many. He also stayed involved in the film industry, making his directorial debut for *In the Gloaming* because he was still passionate about being creative and acting.

Sometimes our life-changing moments provide opportunities for us to do things we never even dreamed about or imagined. As Christopher said and lived through his actions, "Once you choose hope, anything is possible."

One of life's constants is that life changes. Some changes are thrust upon us. Some changes happen organically. Some are influenced by our decisions, like if we get married or have children, or how we take care of our health or spend our money. But even when we have those times when life feels perfect and we wish time would stop, life still changes.

Three of the most common changes that impact us are:

- **Cultural changes**, which result from when our society advances through innovation, invention, discovery, or global events.
- **Loss**, which happens when we no longer have something that was meaningful to us.
- **Life phases**, which are most often associated with our age and the experiences that we go through between infancy to late adulthood.

Cultural Changes

Changes on a cultural level usually occur when things transform for a large group of people. A memorable one for me was when the laptop emerged as the new technological advancement to make us more efficient, especially at work.

As a traveling sales rep, I had a home office. Each rep was

given a big desktop computer. On a field ride with my boss he enthusiastically said, "The field team will be getting laptops soon. When you travel, you'll be able to enter your notes from that day's appointments in the evening."

Normally, we'd be in the field for one week, and then the following week we would work from our home office. During that time, we would enter our notes into our accounts from the previous travel week and schedule new appointments for our next travel week.

Our current system worked fine for me. I thought, *Do they want me to work all the time?* I politely told my boss that I wouldn't be carrying a laptop with me on my business trips and entering notes at night in my hotel room.

Well, about a year after receiving my laptop, I couldn't imagine going on a business trip without it. And today, I can't imagine not having my iPhone, or as the Apple salesperson called it a mini-computer, with me at all times so that I'm able to access my email, the internet, and social media anywhere.

Part of my happiness is now connected to the *convenience* of carrying a computer in my hands virtually all the time, when at one point I couldn't imagine taking one with me on a business trip.

Now practically everyone carries a smartphone with them. Culturally, our phone usage has changed, and our happiness surrounding our phone habits have changed. These phones provide more than a tool to have a conversation. They are a *convenient* way to stay in touch with your family, friends, and work connections with text, emails, and apps; look up directions on command; or entertain ourselves when we wait somewhere.

Like all things, if you don't moderate your usage, it can lead to unhappiness. In the case of your phone, it can distract you from having actual conversations with your friends and family when you are together. Sometimes you spend so much time trying to capture a moment with selfies that you're not really present for the moment. And your phone can be downright dangerous and distracting when you drive.

However, sometimes you don't know that something makes you happy until you have it. New options can change your happiness because you change with them and most often result from innovations, inventions, or discoveries.

- In 1969, we watched Neil Armstrong walk on the moon on bulky or tiny black-and-white TVs with only a few available channels. Now we have hundreds of viewing options, including large flat-screen HD color TVs or small portable devices.

- Prior to the 1990s, most paper communication happened through the post office. As the internet and our mobile phones advanced, our communication changed with email, texts, instant messenger, apps, and social media. Now we send and receive in only seconds communication that once took days.
- After September 11, 2001, the way we flew changed. There are passenger watch lists. The cockpit door on the plane is locked. We take off our shoes to go through security, and bags are extensively checked—and we can only take travel-size liquids on the plane.

Needless to say, the pandemic created huge cultural changes. People alive now will forever view viruses through a different lens because we've experienced how dangerous they can be. Some people may never shake hands again. However, the pandemic also reminded us that no matter what, we are connected to one another. And it has forced us to shift our mindset to live in the present because for a time it was difficult to make plans even a few days out.

In 1999, the Society of Happy People did a survey of the Happiest Events, Inventions, and Social Changes of the Century. Indoor plumbing barely surpassed air conditioning for the top spot. But these inventions certainly changed our culture for the happier.

To make this concept more personal, list five cultural changes —innovations, inventions, discoveries, or global events—that changed your happiness in your lifetime:

1.
2.
3.
4.
5.

When big changes happen, only a few people are considered early adopters. They stand in line for the newest gadget, try the latest social media platform or app first, and eagerly wait for the next big thing. A little later, the majority of us adopt the most popular innovations. And then some will be late adopters and a few may not join in because they are often content to keep things the same or the way they were.

We all adapt to cultural changes in our own time. But eventually we adapt, and most of the time they do make our lives better.

Loss

A friend we'll call James had worked for the same FORTUNE 100 company since he'd graduated college. He'd kept his job through many of the company's reorganizations and layoffs over the years. But after twenty-plus years, a layoff finally included him. At this point, he managed a sales team, and when the displacement announcement was made, the first thing he wanted his team to know was that their positions were all safe. When someone asked him about his position, he simply responded, "That's still being worked out."

A couple of days later his displacement was announced. Although his mind knew how these things worked, and it wasn't personal, it still felt personal. His career and this company were part of his identity. He had to work through all the emotions associated with the loss: anger, denial, bargaining, depression, and finally acceptance. He quickly landed another role with a competitor, but that organization's culture didn't feel right to him. James eventually decided to do one of the things he loved most about his manager job: recruiting talent. As a recruiter, he created a new career normal, one that also made him happy professionally.

When we think of loss, our mind often goes to the ultimate loss, the death of a person or pet. But other losses are also painful and life defining: Relationships with spouses, significant others, estranged family members, or friends. An unwanted job loss. Retirement. Empty-nest syndrome. Downsizing your home. Health changes. Or, as we have learned during the pandemic, even the loss of our normal routine. When we lose something that we valued, we either knowingly or unknowingly grieve it until we find our new normal.

Even if a loss is inevitable or expected, it doesn't matter how prepared we think we are for it; we never really know how we'll feel about it until it happens. All losses require us to find a new normal or reinvent ourselves in some way. They leave a void in our mind, heart, and soul that must be filled with something, even if that something is despair while we're figuring out what our new life is going to look like.

My mom died unexpectedly in September 2004, so when Christmas came around, I was barely thawing out from the shock of her death. Since I'd spent every Christmas except for one with her, I knew that the first one without her would be hard. My expectations were low, maybe nonexistent. I knew that it wasn't going to feel normal or even happy.

My mother and I had always filled stockings, but now that tradition would be forever gone. Our homes always resembled the ones in a Hallmark Christmas movie. Since we lived five hours apart, we would decorate every room while talking to each other on the phone—and I mean *every* room, including the laundry room. That year, I didn't want to decorate at all. I just wanted to hibernate like a bear between Thanksgiving and New Year's Day, and then emerge when the holidays were over.

I felt a hole in my soul larger than I could have imagined possible, but eventually I decided that not decorating would be refusing to honor my mom's memory and the many happy Christmases we'd spent together. Her presence, and the child-like twinkle in her blue eyes when she celebrated the holidays, had always made Christmas magical. My friends and aunts tried to make my Christmas happier with invites to holiday events and nicer-than-usual gifts. I even went on a little holiday shopping spree. On a whim, I decided to hang my childhood ornaments that my mom had hung on her tree. Since my usual big tree was themed with purple, white, and silver ornaments, this meant I had to buy a new tree, and even new glass-blown multicolored ornaments, starting a new tradition for myself.

My brother and I went to see our dad and his wife that year for Christmas. They had a poinsettia and yummy food but no tree or stockings. It didn't feel like Christmas to me. They went to bed early, so my brother and I went to see *Christmas with the Kranks*.

While I was trying to focus on the movie, my mind kept screaming, *This can't be my new Christmas normal!* I almost burst into tears during the film but wanted to stay strong for my brother.

When I finally got back home late afternoon on Christmas Day, my boyfriend came over, and we sat in front of my newly decorated tree talking about our future house and the room I'd decorate for Christmas. He wasn't really fond of wall-to-wall Christmas décor, and I didn't feel like having that discussion at that moment.

I realized that finding my new Christmas normal without my mom would be by trial and error. That year felt like a big error, but as I fell asleep with the hope of future Christmases with my boyfriend, I had a tiny feeling of holiday happiness.

I realized that future holidays might fall short of the happiness I once experienced around them, but it didn't mean I wouldn't have different happy moments. I just had to make an effort to notice them. I still loved Christmas—it was part of my DNA, inherited from my mom. In hindsight, the happiness I felt that holiday was more than I anticipated. Life had changed, but I still experienced happiness even if it was different from my past happiness.

Today I continue that tradition of adding blown-glass ornaments to my even bigger tree. It's part of my new Christmas normal, and I think of my mom every time I decorate. It's one of the ways she stays in my heart.

The timeline to find your new normal varies depending on the type of loss.

Here are a few common losses. If you have experienced any of them, think about how long it took to find your new normal:

- Have you changed jobs? How long did it take for your new job to feel part of your normal work routine?
- Have you moved to a new city or neighborhood? How long was it before that new city or neighborhood felt like home?
- Has a friendship with a close friend ended? How long did it take to find a new normal without that friendship?
- Have you had a health issue that required a lifestyle change? How long did it take before that change became habit?

Most importantly, during any of these changes, did you still have moments of happiness in the journey to discover your new normal?

It usually takes more time to create your new normal after you lose important people through death, divorce, empty nesting, or fallouts. New normals or traditions aren't created by doing them once. New traditions don't replace the beloved old ones, but ultimately you begin to cherish the new traditions, and your old traditions become welcomed nostalgic memories.

While filled with mixed emotions, when a job loss is followed by a new job, this creates a new normal with a new routine, new people, new goals, and new reasons to be happy.

Cultural losses, like the kind after 9/11 or a global pandemic, change us and some of our cultural norms. Before 9/11, no one would have imagined taking their shoes off at the airport to get through security. Now it's normal and expected. Prior to the pandemic, very few imagined not shaking someone's hand.

Losses are part of life. Some leave permanent scars while others leave wounds that heal quickly. When we are at the height of our grief over a loss, it understandably reduces our happiness—and it should. Our heart and soul need to heal. But eventually, a new normal emerges. We adjust—and one day we find ourselves randomly smiling or laughing because we feel a new happiness.

Life Phases

In the movie *City Slickers*, Mitch Robbins, played by Billy Crystal, addressed his son's elementary school class with this memorable and mostly accurate speech about life phases:

Value this time in your life, kids, because this is the time in your life when you still have choices, and it goes by so quickly.

When you're a teenager, you think you can do anything, and you do.

Your twenties are a blur.

Your thirties, you raise your family, you make a little money and think to yourself, "What happened to my twenties?"

Your forties, you grow a little potbelly, you grow another chin. The music starts to get too loud, and one of your old girlfriends from high school becomes a grandmother.

Your fifties, you have minor surgery. You call it a "procedure" but it's a surgery.

Your sixties, you have a major surgery. The music is still loud but it doesn't matter because you can't hear it anyway.

Seventies, you and your wife retire to Fort Lauderdale, you start to eat dinner at two, lunch around ten, breakfast the night before. And you spend most of your time wandering around malls looking for the ultimate in soft yogurt and muttering, "How come the kids don't call?"

> By your eighties, you've had a major stroke, and you end up babbling to some Jamaican nurse who your wife can't stand but who you call Mama.
>
> Any questions?

Our life phases are some of the biggest natural changes that we go through, usually connected to chronological age and the experiences associated with it. We have little or no control over the aging process, but we do have control over how we experience it and some of the experiences during those life phases.

You change daily as a baby, and weekly through toddlerhood, and then noticeably every year between childhood until your early twenties. During those years you rapidly change physically, emotionally, and mentally.

Your life then changes based on your decisions about your career and significant relationships, and these experiences are often interconnected. Did you go to school so that you could pursue a specific profession? Did you move for a specific job? Do you travel for your job? Are you single? Are you with a life partner? Do you have kids? Do you help your parents or grandparents? Do you spend time with friends?

For parents, happiness changes as their family circumstances change. New parents often rate their happiness in early months by how much sleep they get. Then, once toddlerhood arrives, that happiness gauge changes to being able to spend five minutes in the bathroom alone. Once kids become teenagers, parents are happy when they get to have a nice meal with them.

Eventually, those who raise families enter the empty-nest life phase, where their happiness is impacted more by what's going on outside their home than what is happening within it.

My friend Kristin is a recent empty nester who had been concerned about the transition.

"Nonstop activities and events led up to my son's graduation," Kristin said. "It included the senior sports banquet, senior prom, senior field day, and senior pictures. I was both excited and apprehensive: excited that my youngest child was about to embark on a new journey at a great university and apprehensive for the empty nest that was on my horizon.

"I'd heard from many friends that this new phase was a lonely place, one filled with too much time, and a longing for days that had passed. After raising three children, I didn't know what to expect from an empty house. After a busy summer filled with college orientation, family trips, and packing for college, it was finally time for my husband and me to take our son to his new school three and a half hours away. And then we'd come home, without him.

"We'd done this twice before with our daughters," Kristin continued. "But we knew our son was still home, which always gave us comfort. This time was different, and I didn't know what to expect. While I have a part-time job working three days a week, am active at my gym, and have plenty of friends, I still worried that I'd be bored and restless.

"Well, I was wrong. My husband travels several weeks a month for his job, and because our son was home, I hadn't been able to go on those trips with him. But now I'm finally able to join him on business trips. I joined a Bible study and a book club, and I volunteer with an outreach program for teen moms. I was also close to a group of moms who all had kids my son's age, and we regularly get together for lunches and dinners. I also love taking care of our two dogs."

She and her husband enjoy biking and long walks with and without the dogs. While they miss their kids not being home, they are thrilled when they visit. Instead of being lonely or bored, both parents are enjoying their empty nest.

Age-related health challenges also bring changes.

After my dad's wife, Kay, retired, she and my dad built a new home. They had been married for twenty-three years and had lived those years in my childhood home, which was built in the early 1900s and had become a major fixer-upper. The house was on a couple of acres, so it had always been my dad's dream home because it had space for his workshop. But eventually he realized they needed a house with less maintenance, so it was time to build Kay's dream home.

About a year after they'd moved in, my dad was diagnosed with cancer and passed away fourteen months later. Although they had four kids between them, the closest any of us lived to Kay was three hours away. After my dad passed away, Kay wasn't ready to leave the house she loved and her friends.

She spent the next year and a half traveling. On her last trip to Las Vegas, she fell and broke her pelvic bone when she deboarded the plane. When she was released from the Las Vegas hospital, her son took her to finish her rehab in Tulsa, where her daughter lived.

After her rehab, she went back home for a few weeks before deciding it was time to move to Tulsa to live near her daughter. Although Kay acknowledged she was making the move sooner than she'd have liked, she also knew that because her health had changed, so had her needs.

Instead of being angry, she embraced the change. She moved to a community that offered independent, assisted, and full-care living. She got an adorable two-bedroom duplex. She started volunteering at the community library to meet new people. She now lived closer to the casinos she'd taken trips to visit, so she enjoyed going to them more often. She also got to spend more time with her daughter and son-in-law, who lived nearby.

She could lament about not getting to stay in her dream home longer and missing her friends, or she could embrace her new experience. One mindset would create unhappiness; the other, happiness.

Our life-phase changes happen whether we want them or not. We often have minimal or even no control over them. But we do have control over our attitude about them. Do we resist the changes? Or do we embrace them?

Part of embracing our changes means that we notice and experience the happiness during each phase of our life.

Let's look at each of the decades you've lived and recall one or more of your happiest memories during that time:

Childhood
Teens
20s
30s
40s
50s
60s
70s
80s
90s

You may have fond memories of your youth, so you always remember that period as a favorite time of your life, partly because you had fewer responsibilities. But each phase of our life can have equally significant but different fond memories.

You then spend certain years focused on your career and creating a family. The happiness during these years is often marked by your professional achievements and the love and good experiences that you share with your friends and family.

Eventually your life is defined less by your career and more by your changing health, finances, and relationships. Your happiness during this phase is often about your acceptance of and adjustments to these changes.

Then one day you'll reach an age when you attend more funerals than weddings. Your happiness during this phase includes many nostalgic memories. You realize that life is short, so it's important to embrace every happy experience that you can *while you can*.

Some of your life-phase experiences result from your choices, but many happen as a result of natural life cycles. During each phase of these changes, there is new and different happiness to be experienced. It means staying present so that you can feel the happiness that surrounds you at any given moment.

EXPERIENCES

Our experiences are collections of moments that are just part of life, so we may not pay much attention to the individual actions, words, and thoughts that make up an overall experience. Because of each experience's complexity, we usually only glean the lessons after we've had some time to reflect. The important experiences are the ones that inspire changes in our perspective and ultimately influence our future happiness.

Sometimes our experiences allow us to come full circle and find the happiness we thought we had lost.

When she was fifteen years old, Genny moved to England from Sierra Leone, West Africa. "I've always seen people happy," Genny said. "Even when people don't have anything, they're happy. And as children, playing around, even when the rain comes down, you hear the music of the rain on the path, you feel really, really happy. So it was little things like that that made me happy growing up. After I moved to England, I was a little sad because it was so different. Eventually, I got married and was blessed with two sons. But things took a turn in my early forties. I decided to divorce. My house was going to be repossessed. I had two small kids to support. I lost my smile, I lost my confidence, I lost my reason for being.

"I'd go out in the morning and pretend everything was fine. However, coming back home, there was that deep sadness within me. The only thing that made me happy was seeing the kids at night. I was depressed for about five years. I couldn't even look at myself in the mirror, so I took all the mirrors out of the house. It was sad.

"Then one day," Genny shared, "my mom asked, 'Oh, my goodness, I want my daughter back. You used to be so happy. What happened to you?' I started thinking, *What* did *happen to me?* Then I started searching, got myself some help, and was determined to get myself out of this. I trained to be a life coach. I searched for happiness. Eventually I came across your site and was, 'Oh my, a Society of Happy People.' I started following you and wanted to be part of this happiness movement. I decided that I was done feeling so unhappy. I need to do things for myself to be happy. I also wanted to help other people be happy. I realized I had a purpose and a message from my pain that could help others. I thought I could use my pain to help other people.

"So when people see me happy or dressed up in my happy outfit, they say, 'Have you always been like this?' I always tell them the backstory and that you see me now as a happy person, but there were five years when I wasn't happy," Genny explained. "I've come full circle because back home they used to call me Miss Sunshine. So I had it in me. During that five-year period, it was temporarily hidden. I suppose it's like when you look at night when the sun goes down and the moon comes up. So there was that period where I had to be in that to find myself again. And now, the older I get, the more childlike I've become. I want to splash in a puddle or listen to the rain."

My friend, who we'll call Tonya, had worked as a director of marketing for a horrible boss for almost five years. Her boss had really beaten down Tonya's self-esteem, but she finally applied for a job that she thought she'd love. She interviewed, and that company called her boss for a reference. She overheard her boss give her a bad one, and she didn't get the job. After that reference phone call, she was called into her boss's office and asked why she was applying for jobs. She went home that night in tears. She wasn't sure how she'd find a new job if her boss was going to give her bad references. On a whim, and already feeling like a failure, she quit. She called a recruiter she'd met and told her she'd decided that she wanted to be an administrative assistant. The recruiter was wise, knew Tonya's old boss, and could tell she was simply burned out from a bad experience.

The recruiter told her that she'd get her some temp jobs, and in ninety days if she really wanted to be an administrative assistant, she'd get her placed. Tonya agreed and started temping almost immediately. Well, that recruiter was right. It didn't take Tonya long to realize that she really didn't want to be an admin. In a few months, Tonya landed a new job doing marketing. And, in hindsight, she was glad that the recruiter had been wise enough to not let her make a wrong career decision based on part of a bigger experience.

Experiences are a collection of many moments that thread together life's lessons. Although numerous experiences can change us, the most common ones are connected to our *health, relationships,* and *careers*.

Health

Our health happiness can be affected by anything from a minor injury to something serious. Even mostly healthy people navigate colds, flu, toothaches, cuts, or sprains. Many people manage ongoing health challenges such as arthritis, diabetes, high blood pressure, or high cholesterol. Others live with more complicated health challenges such as cancer, heart disease, depression, or multiple sclerosis (MS). Our happiness mindset determines how we handle anything from a minor health challenge to a major one.

One of my favorite books, *Tuesdays with Morrie* by Mitch Albom, is about a professor's last teachings after being diagnosed with amyotrophic lateral sclerosis (ALS). One of the passages from that story beautifully describes how Morrie's changing health altered his happiness measuring stick:

> "Mitch," Morrie said, laughing along, "even I don't know what 'spiritual development' really means. But I do know we're deficient in some way. We are too involved in materialistic things, and they don't satisfy us. The loving

relationships we have, the universe around us, we take these things for granted."

He nodded toward the window with the sunshine streaming in. "You see that? You can go out there, outside, anytime. You can run up and down the block and go crazy. I can't go out. I can't run. I can't be out there without fear of getting sick. But you know what? I appreciate that window more than you do."

"Appreciate it?"

"Yes, I look out that window every day. I notice the change in the trees, how strong the wind is blowing. It's as if I can see time actually passing through that windowpane. Because I know my time is almost done, I am drawn to nature like I'm seeing it for the first time."

I've needed crutches more than a few times. I'm a klutz; what can I say? And every time I did, the inside of my upper arms bruised, and my hands got sore. Yet each crutches experience always reminds me of how easy it was to walk without crutches, a happiness that I normally take for granted.

Our health happiness is complicated. Many health challenges result from genetics; others, from lifestyle or an accident; and some, from aging. Some are temporary; others are long-term. It's easy to think nothing or little about getting a cold or minor cut. We know from experience that even though these things are annoying, they heal, and eventually we forget about them. Our challenge with health happiness usually happens with bigger issues that require lifestyle changes to manage, like when we get diagnosed with high blood pressure and our doctor wants us to lose weight, exercise, and cut out salt. That affects what we eat and what we do, and the changes aren't usually temporary. If we get a more difficult diagnosis such as cancer, although it might be treatable, it reminds us of our own mortality, and we know the treatment won't be easy for us to do and our loved ones to see us go through.

As you review your health history, let's consider some of your health challenges.

Health Challenges	Temporary or Ongoing	On a Scale of 1 to 10 How Much Did It Impact You?	Did You Learn Anything from the Experience?

At some point our health will probably affect our happiness. We're not going to feel happy about a health challenge or what we have to do to manage it. That's okay. We just don't want to get stuck only noticing the challenges. Even during difficult health times, we'll experience moments of happiness: we'll laugh when we watch a funny movie, we'll feel the love of our friends and family supporting us, and we'll probably learn some things about ourselves, including our resilience.

When we aren't feeling well, we may have to make an extra effort to notice these moments. But it's so important that we do because we need the happy times to help balance out the challenging ones.

Relationships

Relationships are possibly the single most important factor affecting our happiness. However, even our most significant relationships are fluid, complicated, and constantly changing. No one is required to like us or stay in a relationship with us, and vice versa.

What's more, one relationship change can have a ripple effect on our other relationships. If we have a disagreement with someone in our friend, family, or work circles, that can affect other people in the same group.

In my early twenties, a friend told me, "All relationships have a beginning, a middle, and an end. A wise person realizes what stage each relationship is in."

Idealistic me thought she was being a bit harsh. Now, the older and wiser me recognizes the truth in her statement. In the middle of even our closest, most authentic relationships, we experience ups and downs and changes based on current circumstances.

Your relationships are ever-changing, not just for you but also for the other people. What goes on in each of your lives individually impacts the relationship. Sometimes you simply end up in different places. Relationships are a dance, and sometimes we are dancing to different songs in different places on the dance floor.

Occasionally, life may take you and an old friend in different directions. You may not be in touch for an extended period of time other than on social media. But one day you reconnect and resume a more engaged relationship. The relationship pause was simply the middle, not the end.

Some people meet their life partner and create a family early in their lives. Others may have several significant others, with a series of unhappy endings, until one day they meet someone with whom they can create the right relationship. And yet others never meet a life mate, not because they didn't want to or didn't try, but because it just didn't happen. And some people are happy being single, with bountiful and rewarding friend and family relationships.

One of my friends, who we'll call Judy, tried to find love, to the tune of marriages with three men who were fun dates but not husband material. After her last divorce, which was financially painful, she moved out of state to live with her sister. A few months later, a friend set her up on a blind date, even though Judy wasn't really looking to date and certainly wasn't seeking a husband. However, a couple of years after that blind date, she married that man and they stayed married for twenty-six years until he passed away. Although it took her a few tries, she finally enjoyed a stable marriage. She had kept her heart open to the possibility of a good partnership, and most importantly, while she wasn't looking for a husband, she didn't close the door to one if the right man showed up.

Some single people create their own families.

A friend, who we'll call Heidi, wanted to be a mom. She dated for years, hoping to meet and marry Mr. Right so that she could start a family. That plan didn't work out for her, so in her early forties she decided she'd do the next best thing: she became a foster mom to two brothers. It didn't take long for her to realize that those two boys were meant to be hers. She adopted them and created a family of three.

Our connections with other people are a reflection of who *we* are at any given moment in our life. When we change, our existing relationships change. We meet new people and start new relationships. Old relationships may pause while some find their natural ending.

Relationships are fluid because even the ones that have a constant presence in our lives evolve and change. This isn't always easy because it's a change we are coordinating with someone else. Our happiest relationships occur when we respect these changes and we choose to grow together. But while growth is constant and inevitable, it's not always easy.

Think about how change has impacted some of your relationships:

- How many best friends have you had over the years?
- Have you had relationships that paused and then reconnected as if the pause hadn't happened?
- Have you ended relationships but still miss these people?
- Have you stayed in a job because you had so many friends at work?
- Have you ever met someone you initially found annoying and only later developed a meaningful relationship with them?

- How have your relationships with your parents changed?
- How have your relationships with your kids changed?
- How has your relationship with your significant other changed?

Our relationships change because people change. The happiness we find in our relationships is dependent on our willingness to let them grow. Most people we meet fall into a neutral category. We don't have a strong feeling of like or dislike for them. However, there's a smaller yet more significant group of people whom we either really like or dislike. Our relationships with these people help us grow, change, and even discover new happiness.

Career

Our career is how we support ourselves, but careers also can define our identity and purpose. Since work is how we spend a lot of our time, it should be a big part of our happiness.

"My career has taken a number of detours," said Jennifer. "I found different types of happiness during each of them.

"By the time I went to college, I knew that I wasn't cut out for my childhood dream of being a vet. I wasn't a fan of blood or organs. I got a degree in business and didn't know what I'd do with it. But after college, I got a job doing inside sales for a large international company. I did well and was able to earn my MBA because of their tuition reimbursement program.

"I'd been in my sales role for more than eight years when I volunteered to be my team's liaison for meetings regarding a major software transition," she continued. "Eventually, that project needed a formal project manager. I was interested in the position, and my company leaders wanted me in that role. It was a win-win. If I hadn't volunteered to be my team liaison, I'd have never gotten the job as a project manager and discovered that I loved it. My inside sales job took me to a new position that I liked better: software testing, where I trained the new users and became the project spokesperson with upper management."

Jennifer spent two years in that role before making her biggest career change: stay-at-home mom. And she's loving that, too.

Careers evolve to meet the needs of our personal life and goals, as well as the economy. The days of working for one company that provides professional growth and long-term security followed by a nice pension or retirement are gone for almost everyone. The industry we work in may change. We may decide we need to make more money, which motivates us to change careers. We may decide we want to change jobs or careers for any number of other reasons. Our careers always evolve.

"Twenty years ago, I was a young whippersnapper," Dennis Yu told me. "I wanted to conquer the world. I was like one of those cops just out of the police academy—*I'm gonna bust every single criminal out there because I'm invincible*—that kind of youthful arrogance. And I think that's okay, at that initial stage, when you're getting going. You work really hard and believe in the hustle culture where you can outwork other people. You believe inherently that the old people don't get it. They're just old and stuck. Now I'm the old guy who needs kids to figure out how to use TikTok. I'm still in the cassette-tape, put-your-pencil-in-it-and-wind-it-up kind of generation. That's okay.

"When I wanted to make a name for myself, twenty years ago, I worked super hard," he said. "That's when I built the analytics at Yahoo. I worked so hard. I don't think I'd ever be willing to work that hard again. Then, after ten years of that, after I'd done some things I could put on a career résumé, I realized that in order for me to grow to that next phase, I needed to be a manager. Then I needed to be a business owner. I ran a digital marketing agency and worked with some of the largest businesses—including Nike and Red Bull—doing their ads, websites, all that kind of stuff.

"Now I'm in this next stage, which is more like a mentor-grandfather–business owner role where I want to see other business owners and workers thrive. I'm in the phase that I get to teach. It's nice for me because my happiness is based on seeing these other people thrive."

Careers are ever changing. Our career happiness depends on our happiness mindset. Understanding what you need from your career at any given moment—whether it's a specific salary, professional development, work-life balance, or any number of other factors—determines your ability to find career happiness.

Take a career inventory to help you evaluate your career happiness:

- How many career changes have you had?
- Were they planned, or did you stumble into them?
- Do you like your current job?
- Do you like your current coworkers?
- Do you like the culture of the organization you work for?
- Are you bored with your current role?
- Are you doing what you'd planned to do for your career?
- Do you want your job to challenge you professionally?
- If you could do anything, what would it be?
- What's the one thing you'd change about your current professional situation?
- Have you ever interviewed for another job only to discover you like your current professional situation more than you thought?
- On a scale of 1 to 10, how happy are you with your current job?

Consider your answers. Do you think it's time to explore other career options to increase your professional happiness? Or are you happy exactly where you are?

Sometimes, depending on what's happening in our lives, we want a job that provides some satisfaction, but it's more important for it to be stable, reliable, and easy. Other areas of our life may fulfill our passion or purpose. Sometimes we just need our jobs to support the rest of our life. Other times, we want our jobs to be what enables us to grow and learn new things. It all depends on what your needs are at any given moment. Then, based on your needs and goals, you find your career happiness, even if it's simply being *content* in your current job because it pays your bills.

While we can influence our career, we don't have complete control over it. We'll have jobs we like, dislike, or love, and ones we feel neutral about. Our career will always change and evolve, depending on many shifting factors. However, we should always be willing to explore how we can grow professionally. It is often along the journey to our goal that we find our greatest happiness. And sometimes we might surprise ourselves and find a perfect new job, one we didn't even know existed.

THE UNEXPECTED

As the saying goes, "Man plans, God laughs." This is one of my life mottos, partly because most of my plans never seem to work out exactly like I thought they would. Sometimes they turn out better; other times I'm sure God is having a good laugh thanks to my planning.

"Three things happened in 2009 at the same time that completely turned my world upside down," Rose said. "I felt like my life was over. I ended a six-year relationship that was going nowhere. The restaurant kitchen where I loved working as a chef closed because of the Great Recession. Then my doctor told me I needed to stop working in kitchens forever because the bone-on-bone arthritis in my knees required knee-replacement surgery.

"I had to do some serious soul-searching. I realized that I had a choice: I could either cave under it all or find a way to work my way out.

"I began by being grateful for the simplest things: being alive and still breathing," Rose continued. "I also tapped into my boundless reserves of creativity and discovered a new way to support myself and keep my knees. I learned to build websites, and as the online world evolved into e-commerce, I added online marketing to my skill set."

Although this life-changing trifecta wasn't planned, it simply changed the way Rose looked at what gave her happiness. It evolved over the past decade. Her work in the online world provides her immense satisfaction and joy. She still has her original knees. And she's discovered the happiness of being single. She created a life from the unexpected that makes her heart smile every single day.

The unexpected happens more often than not. Personal and collective unexpected events have the power to change our perspectives as well as our hearts.

But unexpected events aren't always unhappy. Sometimes unexpected happiness occurs with a chance encounter, following our gut instinct, or finding something new that we enjoy.

Collectively, these events can happen when something makes large groups of people happy. The 1980 US Olympic Hockey Team winning the gold medal reminded everyone that anything is possible. Pharrell's song "Happy" got everyone dancing, singing, and smiling. A pandemic reminded us all that technology allows us to stay connected with loved ones for dinners, holidays, and happy hours.

The unexpected events that change you the most are often connected to Happiness Zappers, like an unexpected death, a surprise health challenge, a significant relationship ending, a car accident, or a flood in your city.

Some unexpected moments stop our world for either minutes or days while our heart processes what our mind knows. Consider the assassination of President John F. Kennedy, the space shuttle *Challenger* exploding before our eyes, the events of 9/11 that we saw unfold in real time, or the untimely death of a beloved celebrity or public figure.

Now, we also know that an unexpected global pandemic can change everything for everyone for an uncertain amount of time.

These big moments, even the ones that don't personally affect our daily life, can influence us to stop and reassess what we value and how we spend our time.

Let's discover how the unexpected has impacted you:

What unexpected personal events changed your life?
What unexpected global events changed your life?
Did you find meaning in these events that helped you redefine your idea of happiness?
Did any of these events redefine your pursuit of happiness?

Ironically, the unexpected should be expected. Although expecting the unexpected is an oxymoron, when we know and accept that things will happen that we can't plan for, it actually prepares us so that we can decide what our mindset toward unexpected moments will be. We can either be fearful of the unexpected and even angry when it shows up, or we can accept the unexpected, and sometimes we'll discover that it can take us to a happy place that we never knew existed.

Our mindset determines our approach to unexpected changes. If we cling to the happiness of our past, we can't find the happiness of our future, even if it's a future we didn't ask for or plan. Sometimes these changes happen from a personal unexpected event like a health issue, a relationship ending, or an unexpected career change. Or they can happen when a new normal is redefined for society when an event such as 9/11 occurs or a global pandemic affects everybody.

Even though it is obvious that happiness changes as we change, we often instinctively resist embracing change, and even deny the changes. But the best way to find happiness in the new normal is to acknowledge the change, mourn the loss if needed, and look for the happiness in the present.

Some changes are so subtle that we don't always recognize them when they happen. Perhaps you started a job that you loved when you began. It was new. You had things to learn. But once you've done it for a few years, you might find yourself bored with the tasks of your job. Instead of acknowledging that boredom, you often start noticing other annoyances about the company—your boss or coworkers, for example, even though the real issue is that your job needs to be different. Those other frustrations were probably there already, but when you were happy with your job, they didn't bother you as much or at all. Your happiness was bigger than the annoyances.

That's why when we find ourselves feeling unhappy, we need to dig deep to figure out if we or the situation has changed. Whether the cause is maturity, life changes, experience, or the unexpected, we all change.

Our happiness *should* change as we change; otherwise we aren't growing. Instead, we become stagnant and likely unhappy, but without knowing why. Happiness happens when we embrace life's changes: planned, unplanned, expected, or unexpected.

This poem by Wu Men Hui-k'ai (1183–1260), a Sung-dynasty Ch'an monk, beautifully describes this principle:

Ten thousand flowers in Spring,
The moon in Autumn,
A cool breeze in Summer,
Snow in Winter.
If your mind isn't clouded
By unnecessary things
This is the best season of your life.

Our life is a lot like the seasons, filled with inevitable growth and change. We should fondly remember the past but also let it go, recognizing that there will be happiness in our current season, also known as *the present*. Life changes. There is no disputing that fact, but our happiness about it is optional. And that happiness changes as we change.

Happiness Principle Four: HAPPINESS IS BIGGER THAN YOU THINK

"Are You Happier Than You Admit You Are?" was the original slogan of the Society of Happy People. When I created the Society in the late 1990s, self-help and personal development dominated TV talk shows, talk radio, infomercials, books, workshops, and seminars. Changing and healing from our past was the focus, so it became a topic of general conversation for most people. But they spent more time focused on *anything* that was wrong, instead of *everything* that was right.

At the time, Carolyn Myss, an author and speaker, called our intimacy language *woundology*: instead of trying to heal their emotional wounds and hurts, people bonded together over common wounds.

We shouldn't minimize our emotional challenges or pain, nor should we minimize our happiness. Ask yourself, *Do I talk about my happy moments as much as I talk about my happiness-zapping ones?*

It occurred to me that if I wanted people to talk more about happiness, they needed to recognize all—or at least more—of the moments when they felt good. That inspired me to think about the definition of happiness. What I came up with was that *happiness is when we feel good.*

All happiness doesn't feel the same. We lump a plethora of positive feelings into the word *happy*, so we don't think of happiness as the broad range of feelings it actually is. This limits our perception of happiness, which then makes it easy to overlook all the different types of happiness there are.

Ironically, recognizing the many different types of happy feelings can be complicated—not because feeling good is complicated but because you're often oblivious to all the little moments that make you happy. You often take them for granted, and you may not even notice them.

When I started the Society, therapists used a popular poster titled "What Am I Feeling Today?" that helped clients recognize different feelings. I divided these types of feelings listed on the poster into two categories: those that felt good and those that felt bad. Then I tallied up each category and discovered that the poster identified roughly three feelings that made you feel bad for every one that made you feel good.

That made me wonder: *Shouldn't the poster have identified an equal or almost equal number of feelings that made you feel bad and good?* I started to question if the therapeutic community was inadvertently teaching people to identify more negative than positive feelings.

A few weeks later, I was at a meeting for the organization where I worked. A coworker and I amused ourselves by trying to identify ten types of happiness. We quickly came up with eighteen. And over the years, I added to that list, and it grew to what I now identify as thirty-one types of happiness.

Happiness isn't linear. It's not one-size-fits-all. It's also not stagnant. *Happiness is abundant.* And it's bigger than you think.

The more you feel good, the higher your energy vibration. You'll also feel less stressed, you'll manage Happiness Zappers more easily, and you'll even find it easier to manifest your most heartfelt desires.

Happy moments occur all the time, even in the midst of unhappy ones, because happiness isn't the absence of unhappiness, fear, stress, chaos, and annoyances. To experience more happiness, all you need to do is recognize and acknowledge all of your happy moments when they happen. That's where the Society of Happy People's thirty-one types of happiness helps.

The list expands your definition of happiness, so all you have to do is notice when happiness happens, not to try to figure it out.

You probably won't experience all thirty-one each day. You'll most likely consistently experience the ones that resonate with you the most, but you'll experience them multiple times in a day. Once you start noticing the different types of happiness, you'll start recognizing these moments when they happen more often, which increases how often you feel good.

Since happiness is personal, how you experience the different types of happiness is unique to you. As examples: What amuses one person might not even be noticed by someone else. What makes someone feel content might make someone else feel bored. What motivates one person might stress another. What makes one person feel valued might embarrass someone else.

The stories below aren't meant to define the thirty-one types of happiness. They are intended to give you examples of how others define these types of happiness and inspire you to think of a time when you experienced that type of happiness, too.

Now let's discover how big happiness can be.

AMUSED

"My four-year-old daughter's class was conferencing in with one of their classmates who was in Argentina," said Francisco. "Since the class was in Spain, they were in a completely different time zone than here. It was night there, and daytime here. The kids wanted to know why."

"We're going learn about how the planets work," their teacher responded. "So we'll start with the big bang theory."

Francisco thought, *Okay, well, this should be interesting since they are so young.*

His daughter arrived home a few days later, super excited about the beginning of the universe. "There was nothing in the beginning," his daughter explained. "There were no people, no animals, no plants, but the nothing was really tied together. It was so tight that it went bang. Then there was everything, the plants, the animals, and the people. Everything."

Francisco thought, *Okay, well, that's a nice summary of the big bang theory.*

The next day she had to miss school. "It's really sad that you're not going to get to learn about the beginning of the universe anymore," Francisco said.

"Oh, I know everything about that already," she replied. "There's nothing else to learn."

"I was so amused about how she understood this super-complex subject," Francisco said. "Her concise explanation of the big bang theory encompassed the whole thing in her mind. Sometimes we try to make things too complicated."

In his new job as a manager, Richard prepared to submit his first departmental budget. His boss told him, "Always include absolutely everything you could possibly want in your budget wish list because lots of things won't be approved."

Richard understood that the initial budget list was just part of the dance between the various levels of management. One level would ask for something (even if they didn't really want it), so another level could say no. Richard knew that if this traditional corporate dance didn't happen, then the bean counters would think they weren't doing their jobs.

Richard decided to amuse himself and ask for a hot tub for his office. That would give them something to cut. After all, his boss had told him, "Your budget is your wish list."

Richard thought his boss would see it, laugh, and cut it. But to Richard's surprise, his hot tub request sailed through his boss and three more levels of management. It only had to clear one more level before he'd find himself picking out a new hot tub for his office. Despite his shock, he was getting a little excited about this possibility.

Alas, at the last checkpoint, Richard's request was finally denied. Nonetheless, he was pretty amused thinking about whether a green marble or granite hot tub would look better in his office.

BLESSED

"I found out at a very late age, twenty-one years old, that I was adopted," said Anna-Sophia. "It completely shocked me and changed my life. It kind of flipped my life upside down for a time. But then I started realizing, a lot of my friends are adopted, too. I started talking to them to get their perspective about it. Did they feel betrayed? Did they want to find their biological parents? How did they feel?

"Then I realized that I have it pretty damn good compared to a lot of adopted kids," she continued. "I'm surrounded by love. And my life is literally a gift. My birth mom could have made other choices. It made me realize that my whole life is a freaking gift that didn't even have to happen. So I'm gonna live life to the absolute fullest.

"One thing that helped me feel more complete was getting my ancestry DNA done," she said. "I found out genetically I'm Polish and Russian. It was really fun to know. Now I can look up things about these cultures.

"I grew up in a nice house with loving parents and have been given so many opportunities that a lot of kids don't have," Anna-Sophia said. "I feel extremely blessed, so I want to just give back. I don't want to live a life that's just pissed off and unhappy because I have it so good."

"We had a house fire a few years ago," said Ferrell. "The fire itself was not bad, but the smoke damage was horrific. The insurance company gutted our house other than the external frame, so we basically had to start over."

Ferrell and her husband decided what they wanted their new home to look like. They created storage under the stairs and added a gas fireplace, among other changes. Now when they walk into their house, it's exactly like they want it.

"It all came from this fire that was devastating at the time," Ferrell explained. "You know, we lost our two pups, and we lost a lot of things that we really cherished at the moment. But now we walk in to this beautiful home and say, 'We love living here.' The fire wasn't happy, but the result of it has been because we were able to create a perfect place for us. It was a blessing in disguise."

CELEBRATIONS

Ana the Distracted Gardener, @annastayshaa, on Twitter shared,

> My eight-year-old said in the car today, "Do you want me to throw the confetti in my pocket?"
>
> I responded, "No, not in the car! Why do you have confetti in your pocket?"
>
> The eight-year-old said, "It's my emergency confetti. I carry it everywhere in case there is good news."

"I'm a big celebration person" is how Apryl described herself. "If you've got something you want to celebrate, I'm in. I especially love celebrating birthdays. So it confuses me that some people don't want to celebrate their birthday. At work, I joke with people who don't want to celebrate their birthday, 'Your birthday is really not about you. It's about the fact that the rest of us want cake. Even if you don't come to the party on your birthday, I still want to have cake.'"

Yvette, who goes by "Super Carpe Diem Woman" when she's being silly, has promoted the "Carpe Diem" mantra for over a decade after losing her friend Craig to ALS.

"He was such an inspiration to me," Yvette said. "Despite his challenges, he lived every day fully. In my Super Carpe Diem Woman persona, I share the superpower to live fully and spread happiness, despite our challenges. I want to help people leave behind their insecurities, their need to be perfect, so that they can celebrate living fully.

"For my sixtieth birthday, my kids gifted me with Carpe Diem Day, which is now listed as an official holiday on multiple websites, including the National Day Archives. I was so moved that part of my legacy, which was inspired by my friend Craig, is now an annual holiday for everyone to celebrate."

CHEERFUL

"I was part of the Washington Capitals' Dance Squad, so being cheerful was part of the job," Anna-Sophia told me. "Before and during the game we'd divide into groups. Some of us greeted fans at the front door and in the stands, some of us would run around with the mascot, and sometimes we'd throw out T-shirts. Between our rotations, we'd walk down the hallway, saying 'Hi' to people, high-fiving them, and just smiling. You had to be cheerful because you didn't know when the cameraman was around.

"Then at the beginning of the game, on the ice rink, they have the big rotating neon lights, and the team comes out to entry music while everyone's cheering," she continued. "It's the craziest adrenaline rush knowing that you're literally part of a huge event that anyone in the United States can be watching. I felt so teeny, but it was like the best feeling ever. I loved it.

"I also worked as a physical therapy technician," Anna-Sophia said. "Part of that job is being cheerful and telling people they're gonna be okay—and making them giggle, and talking about what makes them happy and what they do on the weekends.

"I like to spread joy everywhere I go," she continued. "Sometimes it scares a few people, but whatever. I just throw up happiness everywhere."

CONFIDENT

"A friend of mine suggested that I go on *Britain's Got Talent* in April 2012," said Genny. "Although I didn't know what I was going to do, I filled out that application because I thought it would be fun. I got selected and made it through all of the auditions to get on the live show. I'd created a persona, Confident Queen, to help kids gain confidence. So now imagine, I'm all dressed up as the Confident Queen, and I'm the last person to go onstage. Simon Cowell, one of the three judges, saw me and gave me *that look*. It drained me.

"Now, I'm thinking, *No, oh, no, I can't go on*. But to say you're the Confident Queen, you have to *do* it," Genny continued. "So I went on the stage, and Simon was still giving me that look. I was really, really, really, really not feeling confident. But then I thought, *Don't look at him. Look at the other two judges because they seem to be smiling*. I was doing my stuff. I was dancing. I was singing."

Then after I'd finished the first song, Simon said, "Have you got something else to do?"

So I gave him another one. Then he said, "Have you got something else?"

"Yes," I responded. "I was singing, 'If You're Happy and You Know It, Clap Your Hands,' and an amazing thing happened. One of the judges got Simon to clap his hands and sing the song. So when they voted, I was like *Oh my God, he's gonna slaughter me with this. He's not gonna like me.* The first judge said, Yes. The second one said, Yes. The audience was chanting, 'Genny, Genny, Genny, Genny.' And Simon was like, 'I don't know. I'm just gonna say yes.' And everyone, the audience, everyone was clapping and cheering.

"And at that moment, I felt so excited because I went on *Britain's Got Talent* to have fun," she continued. "But to see that strangers were shouting my name and I got Simon to vote yes? Oh, wow. I was just amazed. And when I finished the audition, going out to my car, they had to help me because everyone outside was going, "Genny, Genny." It was one of those memorable moments that helped me lift my confidence. I could say, 'Simon Cowell was really mean to some people, but somehow, he's soft enough that, in the end, I got him to smile. And he said yes. It was just one of those moments."

CONTENT

"I think a lot of us think we have to feel happy all the time," Robin offered. "Contentment is a form of happiness, too. It's like when my boyfriend cooks for us. I go to his house, and while he cooks, we talk, watch TV, and hang out. When I'm with him, I just feel content.

"My kids are both adults, but they both live with me right now," she continued. "We're like roommates. I don't treat them like kids. We enjoy spending time together.

"I'm just content with my life," said Robin. "There were times in my life when chaos reigned. When I was married, I was never content. Now that I've hit my fifties, I *am* content. I have a job I like. My kids are stable, my boyfriend is great, and I'm fine with that. I don't feel I need to make any big changes. I'm very content."

CREATIVE

"I'm about to release a short, three-minute musical on LinkedIn," Alex told me. "There's some acting, there's a little bit of rapping, and singing. And there's a good message. I had to record a lot of music, write the lyrics and other stuff for it. I even wrote this song about my life for it. I decided, *Hey, I'm gonna write a song anyways. Why not have a really strong message, something that I have lived, that can impact other people?*

"I love creating content, storytelling, and producing videos that have a message to them," Alex shared. "I love that being creative is a big part of my job. I'm happy a lot because I do what I love."

"A few days before Christmas, my oven broke," Kari explained. "Because of the holidays the parts needed to repair my oven were on backorder until January. I was hosting twenty people between Christmas Eve and Christmas Day dinners. I had to get creative.

"A couple of friends brought the main dish and dessert for Christmas Eve dinner," she continued. "Then on Christmas Day we fried the turkey, made several dishes in crockpots, and I went to my son's apartment to bake and then brought those dishes back to my house. Even though it was a little unconventional, it all came together wonderfully."

Sometimes creativity is thinking outside the box.

ENTHUSIASTIC

"I'm naturally enthusiastic," I heard from Allyson. "I'm easily excitable in good ways. It doesn't take a whole lot for me to get excited and be happy. I'm just wired that way. And I get that most people aren't.

"There's a group of friends I travel with," she continued. "I'm called the cruise director and am always in charge of our sightseeing because I love to plan stuff. It's so fun for me. A few years ago, we went to Washington, DC. One day, we walked thirteen miles to see all the monuments. My friends good-naturedly kind of grumbled about it, and we were exhausted by the end of the day. But they were just like 'We know that we're going to see a ton of stuff when Allyson's around,' and I'm like 'You don't call me the cruise director for nothing.' But we were just so happy because that enthusiasm was simply contagious and it was a remarkable day."

FUN

"Well, one of the big things that changed my happiness was getting my dog, Bleu," Jovon shared. "Although I had dogs when I was a kid, I didn't pay as much attention to little things like their unique personalities, and how they're really intelligent beings. It's been fun noticing and experiencing that.

"One time, I signed Bleu up for a race that he didn't win," he continued. "He came in second place. He lost because he got distracted. He was being nosy with someone on the sideline. But once he realized that he was in a race, he started running his max speed. He just barely lost. I always tell him that being nosy prevented him from winning the race. It's fun noticing little things like that about his personality."

"During the holidays I try to go overboard with fun activities," said Chantal. "My daughter and I have lots of traditions that make the holidays fun for us. We take the North Pole Express train to visit Santa. We go to a holiday movie with friends. We go to a holiday play. We host gingerbread-house and cookie-decorating parties. We go to a really big church Christmas show. So every weekend in December, we have lots of things planned.

"I try to make the month magical for my daughter. Seeing her expression, her happiness, it's like me living my childhood. My parents worked six or seven days a week and couldn't take off to take me to do lots of holiday activities. So, for me, being able to do so many fun things makes the Christmas season a really happy time for us."

GIVING

Karen explained, "My husband and I are both trained opera singers. That's how we met in college. Now we sing at funerals, weddings, baptisms, and memorial services. When you're singing for those events, there's a joy in providing something that's of comfort or celebration that has nothing to do with you. You're just the voice there to help, and it's not about you. You're not performing for accolades. And that's probably one of the best things about it.

"And singing sometimes can be very stressful. People don't always think about that. There's a lot of rehearsal.

"We sang at a wedding for a bride we'd known since college," Karen said. "We walked out of the church, and all of a sudden people just rushed over to us. It was nice to hear that others, beside the bride, enjoyed it. A man said to me, 'Nice pipes,' and his wife smacked him. It was quite funny."

"We sang at a funeral for a good friend's uncle," she continued. "Our friend was crying, so on the way out I hugged her. She just said, 'Thank you. You'll never know how much that meant to all of us.'"

"I've learned that when I'm giving, it needs to be something that will make me happy to give," Apryl said. "I've given things to family members and didn't get the reaction I expected. So now I give because it will make me happy to give, not because I think someone else is going to be happy to receive it."

GRATEFUL

"I start every day with gratitude," Martha told me. "Every day, before I even get out of bed, I thank God for my warm, comfortable bed, for my warm house, for the health of my animals, family, and me. I start every day happy.

"Years ago, I started thinking more about happiness and gratitude, and that life is worth living. I find happiness in the smallest things. Washing the dishes makes me happy. I love to have clean dishes. I don't dry them because I like to sit them in the strainer. But you know, just the smallest things make me feel grateful and happy.

"There was a really, really hot day the summer after COVID hit," she continued. "My car broke down. I'm thinking to myself, *Oh, no, what am I going to do?* And luckily, it coasted into this empty restaurant parking lot. The sun was beating down, but the restaurant had a covered outdoor patio. I was able to sit there and call the tow truck. They couldn't come for at least two hours. I had a book in my car. So I sat on the patio and I thought to myself how blessed I am, how thankful I am, and grateful and happy that there's this covered patio. If this was going to happen, I've got a book, I'm safe, I'm secure. And I don't have to suffer while I wait for the tow truck. Being grateful helps me see happiness in the smallest things."

HELPFUL

Kami shared that she "left the retail industry after a decade for mental health reasons. Every day I was so miserable. My husband and I talked about it, and he said, 'Do whatever you've got to do,' so I took some time off work. Then, when I was really ready to go back to work, I wanted to do something where I felt helpful. I wasn't having a lot of luck finding anything. I went to the library a lot because I've always been a reader. I learned they were hiring part-time for somebody at the circulation desk. I got the job and ended up getting promoted to full-time and working in youth services, which included doing story time.

"I love interacting," she continued. "It's not even just about the kids. I mean, the kids are great. I love introducing books and reading to younger people. I think it's very important. But a lot of those younger moms who come to story time, they are at home a lot by themselves. So it's really nice to be able to have conversations with them and give them an outlet for somebody to talk to. And just helping people find the right books. I help grown-ups find the right book by doing what I call my book prescriptions. I ask questions to figure out what they might need answered about any given situation, or if they just need entertainment. Then I help them find the perfect book. So it's absolutely the best job. I love it."

HONORABLE

"I went inside the bank to cash a check," Chet said. "When the teller gave me back the money, as usual I counted it to make sure it was correct."

To Chet's surprise, she'd given him more money than he was supposed to have received.

"I handed the money back to the teller and asked her to recount it," he continued. "After doing so, she realized her mistake and profusely thanked me for being honest. She even said if her till had been short that money, she might have lost her job."

Toby told me, "My husband and I wanted kids, but there's a ten-year age gap between us. My husband finally decided he was too old to have a baby. He didn't want to be seventy-five years old when they're only fifteen. So instead of raising a child, we decided to put one through college. We're putting our nephew from Mexico through college.

"We decided that we could financially support him," he continued. "We both love him. He's a good kid. His parents are great. We knew going into this that it was something we wanted to do. Actually, it's also boosted our own personal relationship. We communicate more because we have to talk about our nephew and his needs. Our communication levels have gone up a lot.

"We're creating our own outside-the-box family. I believe that you can only create love for yourself by loving others. So that's important to us."

Caretaking has been part of Rae's life since she helped her great-grandmother when she was nine. Since then, she's helped her grandparents, an aunt, friends, and now her mother-in-law.

Her grandmother said, "When you're in the hospital, no one wants to wake up alone."

Rae took that message to heart. She realizes caretaking isn't about her. "It's really an honor to share my strength helping someone get through an illness, deal with chronic disease, or even be there during their final days," she said. "You can give them peace."

"No matter how hard it is, I'd do it again for each of these people." Her voice broke with tears as she continued. "They know they are unconditionally loved and forever intertwined with my soul. That gives me happiness."

HUMOR

"A friend of mine was giving talks about stress management using humor," Janice explained. "I tried to support her by attending them. I met a gal in the audience who was a nurse at the local hospital. She had started using a humor cart there. I started volunteering with her, and we'd go around the hospital dressed up with different themes to bring some joy to the patients."

One day they were handing out some clown noses when someone came up and asked if they were familiar with Patch Adams. They were. He was in town. They got to meet and visit with him. Janice thought he was awesome. Later, the nurse she volunteered with wrote him a letter, and he wrote back with some ideas and pointers about using humor with patients.

"He told her about going to Russia with volunteer clowns and lots of clown noses," she continued. "He called it his 'nasal diplomacy.' He told her about a little boy who had been burned very badly. The doctors had to peel the dead skin off. It was painful, and the boy was screaming. Patch gave the boy a clown nose. Then he stood at the top of the boy's head and leaned over so they were almost clown nose to clown nose. Then he stared at the little boy, and the little boy just looked in his eyes and stopped screaming and said, 'You're beautiful.' It reminded us that something that simple helped take away the focus of that pain. That's why we did the humor cart.

"After we heard that story, we gave a woman a clown nose to wear to see her dad," Janice said. "She responded, 'I can't be acting stupid while my dad is so sick.'"

"We shared with her that her dad would love to see her happy," Janice continued. "Of course you're sad because he's dying. But at the same time, he wants to see you happy. It helps him. She finally agreed to wear the clown nose in to see him. She came back out saying, 'That was the best thing. He got the biggest kick out of that.' So you just never know when humor can help. And sometimes, it's in places where you wouldn't think it would be appropriate."

"I used to work for a boss who was a tyrant," Terrill said. "One day I made a big mistake on a project we were working on, and he started yelling at me. He said that I alone screwed up months and months of work in just four hours. I felt bad for a few seconds and then responded with, 'See, I really *can* make a difference around here.' Everyone cracked up, even our mean boss."

INSPIRED

"Happiness for me is when I get to help people," Uno shared. "I've had a challenging life. I had cancer when I was a child, and the aftereffects linger. My mom committed suicide when I was young, and my dad passed from cancer. Making people feel better makes me happy.

"I also enjoy photography and art," he continued. "I decided one way that I could help people was to inspire them with a positive Facebook page, so I created one. A friend who is a social media influencer shared it with her friends, and the page started growing really fast.

"Now I spend a lot of time looking for unique stories and art to share. Sometimes, you don't have to do big, grand things to help people feel better and inspire them to make a difference. Sometimes it's as simple as a great picture and telling an inspiring story."

JOYFUL

Karen said, "For me, I don't think it's really sustainable to always be happy. Because we have moments when we're annoyed, and when we're sad, it's so important to be able to express all of our emotions. I have actually tried to work out what happiness means to me. It's not practical to try to always be positive.

"So I decided to go back to the basics—my love for nature—and found moments of joy. I'm working from home in Australia, and I can go to the beach every day. I literally stop and smell the roses. I stop and look at the lady beetle, at the trees, at the baby in the pram [baby carriage]. Joy is about being far more present and conscious, and stopping to acknowledge it. Now I can hear the birds, and I just think, *Oh, how wonderful is that?* That's a joyful moment."

KIND

"I got an email from someone whose grandma had just passed," Paula shared. "She was very close to her grandma. I'd sent her a card in the mail and also an email with a reading in it that I thought she'd find helpful right now. It took her a little time to get back to me, but she finally emailed me back.

"'You bring so much hope and smiles to my inbox,' she replied.

"All I did was remind her of a little nugget," Paula explained. "It's such an easy thing to do: to send someone an email with something personal. It took less than a minute of my time. I felt so much gratitude that she appreciated that one tiny act of kindness."

LOVE

"My husband and I have been married for over thirty years," Sharon reported. "Early on, we started making a point to do something deliberate to make each other happy each day. It's a little daily gift to each other. Every day, I try to leave him something that will make him happy.

"It's little things," she continued. "He's very involved in voluntary search and rescue. I found a heated necklace that I thought would be good for him when he's out in the mountains on a freezing night. I left it for him on the kitchen table with a little note. Also, it's not always about spending money. I leave notes in his lunchbox or create love coupons. Sometimes, it's as simple as a fast-food gift card or a piece of chocolate. It's just something that's a little bit unexpected. I suppose after thirty years, it's a little more expected, but I try to add the element of surprise.

"For me, it may be a back rub, a massage, or filling my tank up with gas," Sharon said. "He does things that make me laugh. Once he came home with coupons for free food he'd won at the voluntary search and rescue. He said, 'Well, we can go out, and we'll go from one fast-food place to the other to pick up our free food, then we'll have a meal.' And it sounds crazy, but I was rolling over laughing because it was the thoughtfulness and the playfulness. The way he presented that to me just made the difference."

"Part of my healing has been accepting myself completely," Cassandra told me. "All those parts of me that I was trying to push aside in my twenties, and maybe a little bit of my thirties. I'm working a lot on my sexuality. Sexuality in society has been pushed away. We deny or repress or put a cap on it. I'm also very optimistic and playful. But when I get angry, people don't like it. I always pushed away that side of myself. So I take those things, and then I look at them and really accept them in me without judgment that being angry is bad, or being whatever is bad. It's just accepting the fact that sometimes you're a bit bad, and it's okay.

"Love is a huge, deep subject, but it all comes from me; it stems from that level of acceptance. If I accept myself absolutely, completely, and fully, then I'm also able to accept those parts in other people. If I repress those parts and judge them and push them away, then I can't accept them in other people. It's just not how it works.

"Every path in love always has to start with yourself. It's impossible to do it the other way around," Cassandra said. "As a mother, that is huge. When my daughter was almost sixteen years old, she moved back to Australia, even though our family is in Great Britain now. Her dad was saying, 'Now, if you don't study, I'm cutting the money off. If you don't do this or that, I'm cutting it all off. I'm not paying for your bills.' I was the flip side. I'd done so much self-work at that point and had learned to accept all parts of me. So when I looked at my daughter at the airport that day when she was leaving, I said to myself and to her, 'I accept you. You can go, and there's no strings. You don't have to be something for me to love you.' It was a huge moment for me; it was such a profound moment because I then realized, *Oh, holy shit, I've really done the work because I'm letting her go. I'm letting her go with no strings attached.*

"When it comes to my husband, my self-love has helped me drop a lot of expectations of him," Cassandra shared. "I no longer have an expectation of what he has to do to earn my love. So although it's nice for him to do the dishes or buy me flowers, there's no measurement. My changes have made my relationship with my husband filled with more love."

"I decided when I started my company that I would not let my stress or any depression resulting from it impact family, especially the kids," Hema asserted. "I also decided that I'd cook a fresh meal for my kids every day. It doesn't matter how stressed my days are because that gives me the happiness and soul satisfaction that I'm doing something good for my family. It's an act of love."

MOTIVATED

Thomas said, "I started playing tennis when I was nine. Making my high school team was a really big deal because I wasn't the most talented player. I was good, but I wasn't super great. My high school always has one of the top tennis teams in the state, so making that team is really hard.

"I wanted to achieve this goal, so I was motivated to work hard. The first thing I had to do was train a lot more seriously. I had to practice, practice, and practice more, but with a specific intention. My goal was to always be 1 percent better each day. My coach and I always had a specific goal, like improve my forehand or approach to shots. I had to concentrate on those goals and see that progress in motion.

"I made the team on my first try," he continued. "Then I had to work even harder to get my game into the top level just to compete with a lot of the guys who were already on the team. Doing that during sophomore year was a big, big accomplishment for me. And I was really motivated that whole year to compete. I was at practice every morning at 6 a.m."

"Being motivated to work so hard for something gives it different meaning," Thomas said. "I have some great memories of matches, like the ones where it came down to if I won or lost that determined if our team would win or lose the tournament.

I felt I had to win for the team. I'm still very proud of that goal being accomplished. It has had a very big impact on the last couple years of my life."

"When I was a freshman or sophomore in college," Jackson explained, "I was struggling with what I should do with my life. It's kind of crazy that they expect you to figure out your whole life at that age and know what you want to do. Finally, I started to ask, *What* do *I want to do?* and *What* do *I want to study?* instead of *What* should *I do?* One day it clicked. I knew I wanted to study happiness. I realized that if you study finance or biology, it's so that you can make a living to be happy. So why not just cut out the middleman?

"So while I wanted to study happiness, traditional education is about becoming some kind of a skilled employee or a specialist," he continued. "You know, we learn how to show up, take the test, and follow directions, and that doesn't really empower you to be happy. So, I said, *Well, I'll just actually create a major in happiness.* So I might be the first person to ever get a bachelor of science in happiness studies. I also have a major in economics, then created this major that I pulled from psychology, neuroscience, and religious and spiritual practices studies to really understand how we actually live happier lives. As an undergrad, I also created and taught a course in happiness at the University of Alabama.

"One of the things I teach is called Overcoming Myself. It's about forcing yourself to overcome doubt or things that really make you uncomfortable. As an example, the other day I went into my four o'clock yoga class. I've been doing yoga once a week for a few months. I'm not very advanced or flexible. The instructor didn't show up again. Everyone was like 'Time to go home.' And I said, 'Hey, you know, I'll teach the class.' I'm thinking, 'I can figure it out.' Inside, I'm freaking out. But I did it, impromptu, and it wasn't the most graceful yoga class you've ever seen, but afterward, I felt confident because I was motivated to overcome my fears, and there's real power in that."

NOSTALGIC

Seventy-seven-year-old Robert shared, "My wife, Lieu, and I had been married twenty-three years in December. I loved every minute of being married to her. She passed away three days after getting COVID. When I think back on it, how we met always makes me smile.

"Her husband and I were friends from work. He had diabetes that started attacking all his organs. Before he died, he spoke with me privately and asked, 'Could you look after Lieu? Just stop in and make sure she's doing okay. There are lots of things that will be new for her, and she won't know what to do. Just keep an eye on her. She'll be depressed. She'll need your happiness.'

"I've always believed that happiness was something each of us has control over to varying degrees," Robert explained. "There are lots of ways you can lose it. Take me, for example. My first wife and I divorced after a thirty-year marriage and two kids, but we've remained friends. I was always the one who had control over being happy or not. I found that making other people happy really made me happier, too.

"Initially, I helped Lieu move to a smaller place," he said. "I kept checking in on her. About a year later, I was liking her—a lot. So I asked her, 'Would you date me?'

"'No, you're my friend,' she said. 'That's all it's gonna be. I had a great husband and marriage.'

"I asked her another time or two, and she still said no," Robert continued.

One Sunday, Robert decided to show up at her house, in a suit and with a single red rose, at the exact time she went to church. He asked if he could accompany her and made sure to let her know it wasn't a date. To his delight she agreed for him to take her to church. After the service he also took her to lunch.

"Well, when the meal was over, I remember smiling big and saying to her, 'Now that was a date,'" he continued. "So now that you've had a date with me, you really shouldn't say no anymore. She said all right but that we were still just friends and that was all. Well, the next thing you know, I'm in love with her and about six months later I'm asking her to marry me. And, can you believe it? She said no.

"My company sent me to Washington, DC, on business," Robert said. "I asked Lieu to join me, and she did. Unfortunately, she got one of those yucky canned-air colds from flying, so I took care of her for a couple of days while she recuperated. Once she was feeling better, we got to go out and do a bunch of tourist stuff. At one of the tourist shops, she bought me a happy-face button with heart eyes. And under the smile, it said, 'I love you.' I took one look at it and said, 'This is the first thing you've ever given me like this. Does this mean you'll marry me?'

"'Yes,' she answered. 'I really discovered on this trip that I do love you,' she said to me. 'And, I want to marry you, too.'

"When we got married I proudly wore that pin on my suit," he continued. "I'm still trying to be that happy guy she married and carry on what she left me. I'm finding that even though she's gone, she's still here, in my heart. Making other people happy and doing happy things for them: That is what keeps me happy. It ties us together even though she's someplace else."

"My mom had an old, hideous strainer at her house. I love that strainer," Hillary revealed. "It's bright yellow and looks like a long burger basket. I love it because it brings me back to my younger years when I was a kid. I asked my mom if I could have it. Now I'm the proud owner of it."

OPTIMISTIC

"My mother was manic depressive," Karen explained. "Sometimes my home was not a very positive environment. It certainly had an effect on me as a teenager. But I learned very quickly, there were times when I could not be in her world—and I didn't have to be. I could be optimistic on my own and choose not to listen to some of what was going on. As time went on, the doctors understood her diagnosis better, so she was able to get the help she needed.

"She was a neat lady who raised three children, despite all of her issues, worked full-time jobs, and still gave us love and stability," Karen continued. "She provided all the things that you needed from a mom. I was very blessed to have the parents I had, so I looked at it from that direction. Her little singular moments dealing with her issues were not times that should change my optimism about where I was going in life.

"Optimism is huge," Karen concluded. "We specialize in giving forever homes to highly abused dogs that have had horrible backgrounds. Dogs are optimistic. Although it takes some time for them to feel safe again, once they do, they live with so much joy despite their past. That's optimism."

One of my favorite service club creeds is the Optimist Creed, which you can also find at the Optimist International website:

Promise Yourself

To be so strong that nothing can disturb your peace of mind.

To talk health, happiness, and prosperity to every person you meet.

To make all your friends feel that there is something in them.

To look at the sunny side of everything and
make your optimism come true.

To think only of the best, to work only for the best,
and to expect only the best.

To be just as enthusiastic about the success of
others as you are about your own.

To forget the mistakes of the past and press on to
the greater achievements of the future.

To wear a cheerful countenance at all times and give
every living creature you meet a smile.

To give so much time to the improvement of yourself
that you have no time to criticize others.

To be too large for worry, too noble for anger, too strong for fear,
and too happy to permit the presence of trouble.

PEACEFUL

"My first big international trip was twenty-three years ago to Southeast Asia," Sheila said. "We went to a lot of different countries, but Bali impacted me. The people were so peaceful. There's an aura about them that is kind and gentle and peaceful. It was just mind-boggling.

"In the United States, very few people walk around with an aura of serenity. If you stand on a street corner and watch a crowd walk by, it'd be difficult to find one or two people who have the peaceful aura that I saw around all the people in Bali," she continued. "It was amazing, and I still feel peace when I think about that trip."

"I was a victim of multiple child sexual abusers," Rebecca shared. "Even when you want to move past it, it takes time. I spent years in therapy so that I could let go of all that hatred and anger. Eventually, some of my abusers asked me for forgiveness.

"However, one didn't," she continued. "I knew that if I wanted to find peace, I still had to forgive him because forgiveness was about freeing *me*, not letting him off the hook for his actions. So when the day came that my heart forgave him, I wanted him to know that his actions no longer triggered me.

"I got into what I considered the most beautiful, loudest-decorated truck in Texas and drove to Kansas City to tell him, 'I forgive you,'" Rebecca said.

Although Rebecca got the reaction she expected, which was none, she felt what she described as "Peace that passes all understanding." She'd never felt that before. Forgiveness was her key to peace.

PLAYFUL

"I started skipping in 1999, then felt that I should start a worldwide skipping movement and launched iskip.com," reported Kim "Skipper" Corbin. "I recruited head skippers in sixty cities who helped me. After twenty-something years, I still love to skip. It's part of my joy even though I'm not leading a movement in the same way. From time to time, I still meet up with other skippers for events.

"Over time, I realized that my skipping project was about me knowing that I was using my life to make the world a better place," she continued. "Skipping connects me with a sense of play and lightness, and the joy of being. I love to play.

"I have a bunny suit," Kim said. "During the first year of COVID, we couldn't really celebrate Easter, so I made a sign that said, 'Free Hops' instead of 'Free Hugs,' and one that said, 'Honk for Jesus.' I put on my bunny suit, then went hopping around my neighborhood. I made a video of me waving at people that I was able to post. In nonpandemic years, I've passed out candy. One year, a friend dared me to fly home in my bunny costume on Easter Sunday, so I did. I had a tight layover in Atlanta and had to run as fast as I could through the airport in my costume to catch my next flight. People loved seeing the running bunny.

"One day, I wore my unicorn outfit, and my husband wore a big bear head. We went to our local park and walked around to make people smile. I really like this kind of interactive costume play.

"Even at our wedding, our party favors were unicorn horns, so everyone at the reception was a unicorn. It just made it really fun, playful, and magical."

PROUD

"A couple years ago, I started working on creating a more positive mindset and building confidence in myself," Michelle Wax told me. "That led me to do the *American Happiness Documentary* that started the American Happiness Project. I wouldn't have been able to do that without fortifying and really crafting this mindset and belief in myself.

"I spent three months traveling alone. I had zero filmmaking experience. I had to learn how to find people to interview, and all of these different things. There was this two-year time span between the filming and the release of the documentary when I spent so much time working on this project that it's embedded in my soul.

"I knew I'd done the best I could, but it's still nerve-racking to put all this time into something and wait to see how people respond," she continued. "At the premiere and afterward, I received so many amazing notes, text messages, and emails about how much people appreciated the documentary. It was a very proud moment to have so many people all across the country joining me for the online premiere. Then many of the people who couldn't make it to the premiere, but who watched it afterward, sent notes, and that was also heartwarming. Most people don't send notes anymore, so to get even a one-line email or some that were paragraphs long, saying the documentary made an impact for them, made me feel proud of the project."

"I love seeing folks succeed," said Dennis. "It's fantastic. One of my favorite things to do when I wake up in the morning is to check my Facebook and email. I see messages from other people saying, 'Hey, I just want to let you know that I've been following your principles for the last six or seven years, and my digital marketing agency employs forty people. It wouldn't have been possible without the program that you created. I know we've never met before, but I've been stalking you from afar.' These messages feel great."

Dennis told me that it's not uncommon for people he's never met but who know him from his work to walk up to him at airports for selfies, conversations, and to even do what he calls the one-minute video, even though he's not a celebrity.

"When that happens, it tells you that what you're putting out there in the universe is working because other people are being helped, even when you've never met them," said Dennis. "That always makes me feel good and proud of what I'm doing."

RELIEVED

Maureen's dog, Radar, went missing.

"Five days feels like forever," Maureen shared. "I was getting all kinds of different advice on what to do to try to bring him home. Since it was posted on Facebook, people in the area were out looking for him. I'd be out looking for him, and people I didn't even know would say, 'Oh, are you looking for Radar? We're looking for him, too.' And I'd respond, 'Yeah, he's my dog.' It was amazing. It really helped to talk about him. But then I'd come home and cry because he wasn't here. There was a bed and there were his toys, and he wasn't here.

"On the fourth day of his absence, I talked to one of my spiritual mentor friends, who said, 'Maureen, you're focusing on that he's lost. I think it would help you and him if you focus on him being found.' At that moment I was losing hope. But saying positive affirmations about him being found and safe made me feel better. So I said them before I went to bed, when I woke up, and whenever I started getting sad about him not being there, I'd say, 'He's found, he's coming home, he's looking for me, he's on his way, he's home.'

"Then on the sixth day, I got a call from a lady who said, 'We've got Radar here,'" Maureen continued. "I couldn't process it. I literally couldn't process it. Initially, I wasn't sure what she was talking about. Then it hit me, and I was 'Are you sure?' She said, 'He has a collar with his name and your phone number.' I just about fell apart."

He'd been running from people, so Maureen asked if they'd make sure he stayed there. They told her they had him on a leash, and that he was shivering, wet, and cold. He was also huddled up to their dog.

Maureen told them she could be there in two minutes.

"It took me a little more than two minutes, but I've never felt such euphoria as when I got out of the car and walked toward them," Maureen said. "Once he realized it was me, he started wagging his tail. He jumped up when I got to him. He was, like, 'I've been looking for you, Mom.' And I was, like, 'I've been looking for you.' We were both relieved. Which is a big type of happiness."

A woman, who we'll call Stephanie, had a landlord who, after six years, decided that he wanted to sell the home he had been renting to her, so he gave notice that she and her family needed to move. He tried to give them time to find a new home, but after seven months they still hadn't found another affordable home to rent. The landlord finally told them they had to leave over Thanksgiving weekend, even if they didn't have a place to go.

She and her family, including two school-age kids, packed everything up and spent the first week in a hotel. She even had to leave two of their four pets at someone else's house until they found a new home.

The hotel was so expensive that it used up most of their savings, so they didn't have money for deposits on a new place. One of Stephanie's friends offered to let them stay with her so that they could save money for deposits while they looked for a new place to live. After a couple of weeks, they had saved the money needed for a deposit and the first month's rent but were still trying to find an affordable home.

Finally, a home was available, and they applied. Initially, their application was rejected, and Stephanie felt despair. However, she tried to keep a strong outlook for the kids' sake. She decided to call to find out why they hadn't been approved. She was relieved when she discovered an error had been made when processing their application. The landlord reprocessed it, and they were approved for the home.

When Stephanie found out they were approved to rent the house, she'd never felt happier. She was relieved that she and her family were able to start the new year in their new home.

RESPECTFUL

"My mom taught me and my sister that whenever you see somebody on the street, an older person or anybody, you smile and look at them, and say 'Hi,' or 'May I open the door for you?'" Jeff explained. "She reminded us that some people don't have friends and family, and they may feel lonely. She always told us that you never know what somebody is going through, so you might be the brightest part of their day. Always try to connect with somebody. She wanted us to respect everyone."

This philosophy has been part of Jeff's family legacy. In a book his grandfather wrote, he shared that everyone should be polite to people they passed on the street and say "Hi," or "Hello," so that everyone who crossed their path felt recognized.

"Growing up, I was bullied in school," Jeff continued. "I have really vivid memories of the second day of kindergarten when I was bullied and made fun of. I often felt alone in school. I really didn't have anyone to talk to or confide things to. I guess it's always been with me to make sure you treat people with respect and kindness. Try to make them feel happy in some small way."

Jeff's natural empathy toward people played a role when in high school he became aware of the homelessness problem. He'd been selected as a delegate for the American Cancer Society's National Lobby Day and went to Washington, DC. When he was touring the sites one night, he saw the White House to his right, and about thirty feet from him, he could see somebody sleeping on a bench in a garbage bag. It both shocked and scared him. Then, around the corner from his nice hotel, there was a homeless shelter. One day as he was leaving to go to the White House, he saw a guy with part of his leg amputated, eating a chili dog. There were flies and blood around the man's leg. All of this made him angry.

"A few years later, I disguised myself as a homeless person and sat underneath our downtown clock when it was really cold," Jeff said. "Whenever somebody came up to me and helped me in some way, whether it was giving me mittens, a hat, a scarf, money, or even some food, I reached into my little coin purse and gave them either a gift card or cash back. Then I'd explain I wasn't really homeless, and that I was just doing this experiment."

Eventually, Jeff's passion for helping the homeless grew from volunteering to making it his career. He believes everyone, including the homeless, should be respected. After all, being respectful is something his mom taught him.

SATISFACTION

"Happiness for me is both work and personal satisfaction," Rem said. "I'm a very goal-oriented person, so accomplishing something each day—whether it's a small task, a large task, or progress toward a long-term goal—gives me motivation and also makes me feel satisfied.

"I'm always learning something new, whether it's coding, programming, a new way of presenting information, or a new technology. These little moments make me feel successful, like I've accomplished something and am adding value. When I say 'adding value,' I don't mean to the company or to other people. I mean for myself; I feel like I now have this additional skill or piece of knowledge, and that makes me super satisfied and happy.

"I teach online classes at night at two colleges and one university," he continued. "It's extra work. But when I get the positive feedback from the students, those little moments are more important to me than the money, the time, or the lack of sleep because I'm working so late. Those moments motivate me and provide a level of satisfaction that I can't replicate anywhere else. For me, anything that I do, there has to be some sort of satisfaction that I get from it."

"I've spent a lot of time taking care of my nieces and nephews —specifically, making sure they have what they need. When my niece went to college she wanted to stay in the dorm. I was able to financially help with that. I was just in a position to help provide an experience that I couldn't get when I was her age. I did it because I'm her uncle. I have a vested interest in her education and well-being. I can impact people, which gives me satisfaction.

"That's created the next generation to continue that legacy of helping others," he explained. "My niece has been tutoring my younger nieces and nephews—her cousins—as part of home-schooling and distance learning while my sister-in-law and brother work. That's rewarding, too. She's paying it forward.

"My work lives on through others, and the value of that, to me, is incalculable. You can't put a price tag on it. And that's so satisfying."

SOCIAL

"I was really shy, so in my late forties, I made a conscious decision that I was going to overcome my shyness," Robin told me. "I did a couple of speaking engagements in front of 200 to 300 people. I become a marketing director who represented our company at chamber of commerce activities. I went to every ribbon cutting, public relations event, and fun activity that happened in town.

"Once I arrived at an event, I forced myself not to be a wallflower. I decided I'd go up to people and be comfortable with introducing myself and then being sociable with them. So, for me, being social means pushing outside of my comfort zone of being shy and an introvert.

"It made a tremendous difference for my happiness, and it changed a lot of things," Robin explained. "I met my boyfriend because I became more social. I'd been invited to an after-work birthday party. Normally, I'd never go to these parties. I even remember walking up to the restaurant, looking in the window to see who was there, and going back to my car. But I came back and went inside.

"It was so exciting and fun. Then a guy walked in the door. I saw him immediately, and I went, 'Okay, he's here for me.' I actually went up to him and talked to him that night. I gave him a business card, and that moment has changed the past few years of my life.

"Being social also showed my kids a side of me they hadn't seen before," she said. "People around town knew me since I'd been attending all these events. My kids would go somewhere, and people would come up to them and say, 'Are you Robin's daughter or son?' It wasn't like that before I became more social, so being social has definitely changed a lot in my life."

"Your relationship with your children transitions when they are adults," Paula shared, "although you'll always try and guide them if they need you.

"So one thing I started doing a few years ago was a new Christmas holiday tradition. I arranged to go out to dinner with each one of my three children and their significant other if they have one. We'll go to a play or comedy club or an event. Not just a movie, but something a little more interactive. And then we go out to dinner together, and we just spend hours laughing and talking and getting to know one another better as adults, as people—not just as family members. It's become a nice new tradition."

SPIRITUAL

"My parents prayed with me and taught me from an early age to trust God rather than myself, and to look to God for strength and wisdom for any challenges I faced," Amy said. "I learned to never give up because God was with me and I could rely on that.

"I've always engaged my faith and prayer to deal with challenges. It makes my days less anxious and flow more peacefully when I pray and study the Bible each morning. It renews my mind every day. In my mid-twenties, I started writing my prayers in a journal. I like being able to reread them and see how God has answered them."

As a mom of three, including a ten-year-old son and twin girl toddlers, when things get chaotic, as they inevitably will, Amy often stops and says a prayer, trusting that God will navigate them through the chaos. For Amy, she practices her faith through her actions. Her faith is her spiritual happiness, which spills into her daily life.

"I moved to Israel to study," Yaacov said. "Then I met the girl of my dreams and never left. Her family's here. And after we got married my parents and siblings also moved here.

"I'm constantly working on myself to grow more. I always try to be better than I was yesterday. We can easily fall into a routine and forget how to be thankful and grateful. Even if our goal is to be happy, that's something that we sometimes take for granted. I've found that working on being closer to God helps me be happy. It's a type of happiness that doesn't go away as quickly as experiences.

"I could spend time coloring a picture and be happy about it," Yaacov continued. "Or I could spend that time trying to be closer to God, through studying or praying. This helps me interact with others in a way that's spiritual. And by tapping into that love, I become, to a certain degree, a better version of myself. Then the rest of my day changes because I'm just happier going about my daily routine. My day is very different when I don't take time to connect with God."

After Yaacov gets the kids ready for school and drops them off, he prays for about an hour. Then he studies the Bible and Talmud for about an hour. Then he goes to a study group for a couple of hours.

As Yaacov described it, "My morning is very spiritual. I spend probably four or more hours on spirituality. When this routine happens, the rest of the day just flows. Recently, I was feeling a little bit under the weather. I didn't do my regular morning routine. I prayed and studied, but it wasn't as intense. I wasn't as immersed in it as I usually am because I didn't feel 100 percent, and my day was different. I didn't have as much energy. I wasn't as happy. The morning I went back to my regular schedule, it was a different kind of day. I was much calmer, much more in tune with myself and what I wanted to accomplish. My spiritual practice enables me to go through the day in a completely different energy than it otherwise would."

"I got into yoga in my late twenties, early thirties," Debbie reported. "My body was changing. My knees were getting a little bit wonky. I needed to find an exercise that was going to be a little bit gentler on me physically. I was working at a large national fitness center teaching step aerobics and kickboxing.

"I was not interested in the spiritual, mental, or philosophical aspects of yoga at all. All I wanted was to have a nice, low-impact, gentle practice for my physical health. A fitness center yoga class isn't like a yoga studio, where you're also doing more of philosophy of yoga, so it pretty much fit.

"However, in my opinion, after teaching yoga for more than fifteen years, you can't help but get somehow involved in the mental, spiritual, and emotional aspects of it," Debbie continued. "It's the nature of the beast. Now, I didn't know that when I started, and I was determined to keep the nonphysical parts at arm's length. But it captures you. I also had a religious life. Eventually, those two parts of my life—the spiritual part of yoga and the religion that I was in at the time—collided, so I had to make some pretty dramatic changes and choices over the course of a couple of years. It was not easy. It was what I'd call a 'spiritual crisis.'

"I didn't know it at the time, but looking back on it now, I didn't have a lot of peace then," she shared. "I was very judgmental, harsh, and a little intolerant. When I reflect on that now, there's no peace with that. And to me now, that is unhappiness. Whether you know it or not, it's a separation from source. When we judge, that's separation from source and your fellow humans. I was too busy seeing where others were wrong and I was right, thinking, *If only everyone could see it the way I see it.*

"The longer I was going to church, the more dogmatic and judgmental it sounded to me. Eventually, I asked, *Why am I doing this?* My husband and I were dragging our kids every Sunday morning to church. We'd get dressed up, and since we went to a Black church, we were there for three or so hours. Eventually I told my husband that we're not going anymore, and he agreed. At the time, I didn't know what I believed. I just knew that it wasn't making me feel spiritually happy, and I couldn't do it to myself or to my kids either.

"During that time, one of the teachers from the fitness center, who was my yoga mentor, was leaving to start her own yoga studio," Debbie said. "She asked me to come with her. I just took the leap. However, it caused so much internal conflict that I almost quit. I didn't know Buddhism. I didn't know any of that stuff. My mentor said, 'Take what you can and leave the rest.' It was baby steps, and just talking it out, and going out on faith.

"In hindsight, I absolutely 100 percent had to go through that experience to find true happiness. I don't think I would have found happiness without the experience. To me, happiness is peace and contentment with who you are. And yoga helped me find that."

SUCCESSFUL

Admiral William H. McRaven delivered the commencement address to the University of Texas students, class of 2014. This is an excerpt from that address.

> If you want to change the world . . . start off by making your bed. Every morning in basic SEAL training, my instructors, who at the time were all Vietnam veterans, would show up in my barracks room and the first thing they would inspect was your bed. If you did it right, the corners would be square, the covers pulled tight, the pillow centered just under the headboard, and the extra blanket folded neatly at the foot of the rack—that's navy talk for bed.
>
> It was a simple task—mundane at best. But every morning we were required to make our bed to perfection. It seemed a little ridiculous at the time, particularly in light of the fact that were aspiring to be real warriors—tough, battle-hardened SEALs—but the wisdom of this simple act has been proven to me many times over.
>
> If you make your bed every morning, you will have accomplished the first task of the day. It will give you a small sense of pride, and it will encourage you to do another task and another and another. By the end of the day, that one task completed will have turned into many tasks

completed. Making your bed will also reinforce the fact that little things in life matter. If you can't do the little things right, you will never do the big things right.

And if, by chance, you have a miserable day, you will come home to a bed that is made—that you made—and a made bed gives you encouragement that tomorrow will be better.

If you want to change the world, start off by making your bed.

"I was the only woman on the 1996 NYC Marriott Marquis Culinary Olympics Team," Rose said. "Our team of five competed in Berlin, Germany, and we won big: twenty-five gold medals, seventeen silver medals, and six bronze medals.

"It was a dream of mine to compete and win ever since I graduated from the Culinary Institute of America in 1988. It took eight years of laser focus—endless hours of learning, practice, critique, and a burning desire to be one of the world's best chefs.

"Achieving that goal made me feel successful," Rose continued. "I still have a wall full of awards that make me happy to look at and remember that success."

VALUED

"I learned years ago, and am still learning, that people receive appreciation and value differently," shared Justin, a human resource leader. "Some people want praise and recognition in front of a big crowd, and some people would be mortified if you ever did that. So everyone's got their own value language, which is like a love language.

"For me, showing value to people starts with just listening so that people feel heard. As more people have worked virtually, our meetings have become less about socialization, chitchat, and camaraderie, and more about the logistics of what has to get done. I've enjoyed being back in the office because it's easier for me to show value to people in person. My company just moved into a new office space, and I can go check on people and say, 'How's your new desk? How's your new space? Have you got what you need? Is there anything else that could help make your transition to the new office a little smoother?' A lot of times, the answer is 'No, everything's great.' But it sets the stage for them in the future; if they've got a need, they come to me. That's rewarding for me. It wasn't as rewarding doing it virtually because HR is so much more than being on a laptop.

"I feel valuable when I'm helping and serving our employees," Justin concluded. "But it also helps them feel valued that I remember their name, and that they have a kid. It's little things:

treating the different people at the company—from the summer intern to the employee who's been here thirty years to a partial owner—with respect and dignity that's rewarding. I head home at the end of the day feeling valued."

"When I was the private stewardess for the Doobie Brothers back on their 1975 fall tour, we did a concert in Largo, Maryland," Janice shared. "There were about 20,000 to 30,000 people there. It also happened to be my twenty-eighth birthday.

"After they did their whole number, they left the stage and the lights went out. Then people flicked their candles or cigarette lighters, and the band came back out. They also brought out a birthday cake and brought me onstage. Everyone sang 'Happy Birthday' to me. All I could think was *Oh, wow*. Then I got to sit on the stool and play the tambourine to "Listen to the Music." It was so awesome that they were willing to share their limelight with me. It made me feel that they really valued me."

You now have thirty-one types of happiness that you can notice each day, which will raise your vibe and make you feel better. What's the best way to start incorporating these into your happiness mindset?

Start by making a point to notice only one type of happiness for a day, a few days, or a week. Then notice a different one. Otherwise, trying to watch for all thirty-one might feel a little overwhelming.

You'll probably have more amused moments than moments of relief. All happiness isn't equal in intensity or number of experiences. Also, all happiness is personal, so what makes you feel valued is probably different from what makes someone else feel valued.

Your expanded happiness awareness is something that should be fun, so don't let noticing more happy moments become a Happiness Zapper in itself. There's not a right or wrong way to do it. Don't stress.

It's simply about expanding your happiness mindset by realizing that happiness is bigger than you think.

We've included our Happiness Counter to make it easier to track your happy moments. You can also download it from sohp.com/phhc or download the app at SOHP.

> If any of the *Practical Happiness* story contributors inspired you, find out more about them at sohp.com/phc.

Happiness Counter

The Society of Happy People identified Thirty-One Types of Happiness to help you realize how many happy moments are already part of your day.

Pick a defined amount of time—the past hour, four hours, or longer—then mark each time you experience one of the types of happiness below. Then tally up how much happiness you experienced.

AMUSED		KIND	
BLESSED		LOVE	
CELEBRATE		MOTIVATED	
CHEERFUL		NOSTALGIC	
CONFIDENT		OPTIMISTIC	
CONTENT		PEACEFUL	
CREATIVE		PLAYFUL	
ENTHUSIASTIC		PROUD	
FUN		RELIEVED	
GIVING		RESPECTFUL	
GRATEFUL		SATISFACTION	
HELPFUL		SOCIAL	
HONORABLE		SPIRITUAL	
HUMOR		SUCCESSFUL	
INSPIRED		VALUED	
JOYFUL		**TOTAL**	

sohp.com/phhc

LIVING A LIFE OF PRACTICAL HAPPINESS

> In ancient China, the Taoists taught that a constant inner smile, a smile to oneself, ensured health, happiness, and longevity. Why? Smiling to yourself is like basking in love: you become your own best friend. Living with an inner smile is to live in harmony with yourself.
>
> —Mantak Chai

In a realistic way, practical happiness means that by managing your Happiness Zappers and experiencing more of the happiness around you, you'll keep your inner smile.

Our mindset and experiences have the power to unleash the happiness inside us. When we choose to live in the present, feel all our feelings—the good and the bad—and actively look for all the happiness that occurs moment to moment in the complex web of our lives, it's possible to feel good more, smile more, and improve your life so that ultimately you live your happiest life.

If you'd like to get a Practical Happiness Principles poster, go to: sohp.com/phpp.

Would you like a downloadable *Practical Happiness* workbook to help you easily apply the four practical happiness principles in your life? I'd love to email it to you as a "thank you" for your honest review of the book.

Post your review on your retailer's web site, Goodreads, or on social media and send us the link.

Visit http://sohp.com/phreview for all the details!

ABOUT THE AUTHOR

Pamela Gail Johnson became a happiness advocate when she founded the Society of Happy People in 1998. As a mostly happy person, Pamela asked herself, *Where are all the happy people?*

She created the first happiness holidays, which are now celebrated by millions of people worldwide: Happiness Happens Day, Happiness Happens Month, and Hunt for Happiness Week.

She has been a frequent media guest on ABC, CBS, NBC, CNN, radio, and podcasts, and her work has been covered by magazines, newspapers, and online publications.

Pamela's professional experience includes working for the Hazelden Foundation, and for Staples and American Express, in business development, where she received many awards for her sales results.

Currently she's known as the Practical Happiness Advocate, helping people who want to improve their lives by feeling happier.

As a speaker, Pamela does keynote addresses, breakout sessions, and other events.

Visit pamelagailjohnson.com or sohp.com to get more information about Pamela.

ABOUT THE SOCIETY OF HAPPY PEOPLE

The Society of Happy People, founded in 1998, encourages people to celebrate happiness and to talk about being happy when they are.

To encourage this, the Society sponsors three annual celebrations that were the first-ever annual happiness holidays:

- Happiness Happens Day (August 8), which started in 1999
- Happiness Happens Month (August), which started in 2000
- Hunt for Happiness Week (third week in January), which started in 2001

These happiness holidays are celebrated worldwide every year by individuals, organizations, schools, hospitals, and businesses.

Pamela Gail Johnson, the Society's founder, and the Society have been featured in many national and regional magazines and newspapers, including *People*, *Newsweek*, the *Washington Post*, the *Costco Connection*, *USA Today*, *Prevention*, *Parade*, *Harper's*, *Yoga Journal*, *Self*, *Redbook*, *Glamour*, the *Wall Street Journal*, the *Dallas Morning News*, and the *Los Angeles Times*. Numerous broadcast outlets have featured Pamela and the Society, including CNN, ABC, CBS, and NBC; the shows *Good Morning America* and *The List*; local TV network affiliates around the country; and radio stations nationwide, including NPR affiliates. Pamela's work with the Society has also been covered by the Associated Press.

Numerous websites, newsletters, and blogs have written about the Society and linked to it, including NBCNews.com, Ask.com, DailyInBox.com, Huffington Post, Beliefnet.com, and USAToday.com's Hot Site of the Day.

Join the mailing list to get the latest inspiration and activities from the Society of Happy People at sohp.com.